BACKROADS LAW

TRUE STORIES OF SOUTH DAKOTA GAME WARDENS

Compiled and edited by **Jona Ohm** on behalf of the
South Dakota Conservation Officers Association

The South Dakota Conservation Officers Association is proud to present this collection of stories about the inception of our organization, and officers past and present.

This book is dedicated to all the officers who have served over the years, protecting South Dakota's natural resources – especially those who have fallen in the line of duty or passed away early in life. We would also like to extend a special thank you to all the spouses and families who support us in the work we do. We could not do it without you!

Chris Kuntz, President
South Dakota Conservation Officers Association
2017-2018

A Tribute to Conservation Officers

By Spencer Vaa

Spencer Vaa is a former conservation officer, game manager and state waterfowl biologist. He worked with South Dakota Game, Fish & Parks from 1972 – 2010. Spencer originally wrote this piece for A History of Waterfowl Management, Research, and Hunting in South Dakota, *published in 2014. It is reprinted with permission from the author.*

When a landowner, sportsman or private citizen needs to talk to a "wildlife person," he or she is likely to dial up a conservation officer. Conservation officers, commonly called COs (or even the more dated "game warden" title), are the face of South Dakota Game, Fish & Parks (SDGFP).

Why is this? I believe it's because a CO is a person who's involved with virtually all of the activities going on within the department.

One day it might be enforcing game, fish and boating laws along with running a pheasant brood survey. The next day it could be signing up Walk-in-Access area or conducting a youth hunter safety class. The CO becomes well-known by the public in his or her area (usually a county or two) and becomes the point of contact for the department.

I've always been of the opinion that working as a CO is a great way to prepare a person for virtually any job within SDGFP. The hours can be long because the position means the CO is on call 24-7 and will likely be working on the opening day of pheasant, duck and deer seasons.

But the rewards are great because a good CO can make a difference protecting the wildlife resources and delivering excellent services to farmers and ranchers, sportsmen and the general public.

Federal game wardens, more properly titled "Federal Agents," work closely with state COs. I've had the privilege of working with some of these talented men, including former Federal Agent John Cooper, who served as Secretary of SDGFP from 1995-2007. I remember working with John and CO Dan Plut at the McDowell goose pits near Pierre back in the 1970's, when Dan and I were rookies. Now, that was an experience!

To the close fraternity of State and Federal Wildlife Officers – thank you for a job well done!

The Inception and Accomplishments of the South Dakota Conservation Officers Association

By Owen Meadows, May 2018

Owen spent his career as a conservation officer in Hot Springs. He served as a state game warden and then a conservation officer from 1967-2000. In 2018, as this book was in the works, Owen served on the board of the South Dakota Conservation Officers Association (SDCOA) as the representative for retired members. He is also a founding member of the SDCOA. His recollections of the events that led to the founding of the SDCOA are from documentation he kept over the years.

Prior to 1970, wildlife law enforcement was the responsibility of officers referred to by South Dakota law as state game wardens. They functioned in the Division of Law Enforcement within the Department of Game, Fish, and Parks. At this time in South Dakota, fifty game wardens were supervised by one chief game warden and three assistant chief wardens.

In 1970, the Department of Game, Fish and Parks experienced a reorganization. Game wardens were renamed conservation officers. The minimum educational standard was increased to require a Bachelor of Science degree in Wildlife Management or a related field, which also earned a raise in pay. The officer job description was amended at this time to include management responsibilities for game and fish, as well as lands owned by South Dakota Game, Fish & Parks, though many of those efforts were already being handled by game wardens.

Five regions were created in the state. Supervisors and assistant supervisors were put in place in each region for all areas of responsibility including law, game, fish and land. In addition to regional leadership, separate, statewide supervision positions were located in Pierre for fish, game and department-owned land. However, because the chief game warden position was eliminated, there was no centralized coordination position for law enforcement.

As the reorganization unfolded, the changes implemented and the kinks worked out, conservation officers were considering the benefits of forming an association. Though not a union, an officer association could pursue dialogue and changes in the common interest that could potentially benefit officers, the Department of Game, Fish & Parks, as well as the public. It would be a way for officers to speak with one voice.

Conservation Officers had always worked closely with their local police, sheriff and highway patrol, with calls for assistance going both ways. However, the reorganization put the focus of conservation officers on wildlife and habitat resource management and less on law enforcement activities.

Nevertheless, officers were still likely to happen upon situations involving intoxicated drivers, thieves or other criminals. In this case, they would be forced to make a citizen's arrest. This would potentially expose them to greater liability than an average citizen. They were law enforcement, to an extent, and may not have the exception an average citizen may be granted in the event of an unlawful arrest or detainment.

At the time of its inception, the primary concern of the SDCOA was earning peace officer status for conservation officers.

On April 28, 1973, 26 South Dakota State Conservation Officers met in Fort Thompson to discuss forming an association. Examples of constitutions and by-laws were considered by those in attendance, and a discussion was held to determine favorability of moving forward.

The officers present voted to form the South Dakota Conservation Officers Association.

Association officers were elected that day, as were regional representatives. A formal meeting followed, presided over by President Floyd Gaarder. Formalities were discussed and dealt with. Any remaining needs or formalities required to have a functioning association were to be handled by the elected officers.

Very little time passed before 49 officers joined as charter members. The Association held its first statewide meeting in July of 1973 in Pierre, South Dakota.

Some of the changes and improvements achieved by the association's efforts to work with administration include:

- Earning peace officer status, which took three legislative sessions (1973-1975).

- Discussions for improved uniform and badges began in 1973 and were realized in 1978. Additional changes and improvements were made as years passed and will probably continue as long as conservation officers and the association exist.

- In 1975, conservation officers were granted use of South Dakota State Radio's law enforcement channel at night if so equipped. Efforts toward this began in 1973. Eventually, officers received authorization for 24-hour use of the frequency.

- In 1980, officers were issued Smith & Wesson .357 Magnum side arms, along with the associated leather and equipment by the department. Efforts toward this also began in 1973.

- Glock .40 caliber semi-auto side arms replaced the Smith & Wesson .357 Magnums in 1991.

For some undocumented reason in 1992, the wearing of sidearms as a uniform item became controversial. Officers of each region met with South Dakota Game, Fish & Parks Commissioners. Following the four regional meetings, the administration, other employees and the commission came out with improved understandings of why sidearms should always be part of the uniform. The firearms policy was improved at this time.

- Efforts for officers to receive Class B or Law Enforcement Retirement began in 1979 and were realized in 1983.

- Support for efforts to improve officers' employment classification and compensation, 1973-present.

In addition to working with the department in these ways, SDCOA actively works to support outdoor education, students and families.

- Assist outdoor women's groups with events and education 1990's – present.

- Provide scholarships to university students interested in wildlife law enforcement degrees.

- Contribute to and participate in youth hunting activities.

- Assist officers wishing to attend the North American Wildlife Enforcement Officers Association (NAWEOA) annual conference.

- Community service through volunteerism and fundraising for officers and families in need.

As a professional organization, the association continues to work with members to improve the profession, guided by our mission statement:

The South Dakota Conservation Officers' Association (SDCOA) will pursue the highest professional status of wildlife conservation officers and the practice of wildlife law enforcement. This shall be accomplished by promoting effective communication and relationships between the SDCOA, Department of Game, Fish and Parks, wildlife professionals, and other law enforcement agencies.

THE WARDEN

Tonights like lots of others
You've radioed you'll be late
A car on the highway hit a deer
Theres been a lot of late.

I put supper in the oven
To keep it warm for you
Hot or cold, you don't complain
A dry dinners nothing new

As you sit down to eat
The phone begins to ring.
Someone wants a license, or
Where are the fish biting?

Seasons come, and seasons go
They march clear through the year
You get called out in the night
Some ones shinning deer.

You say your works your hobby
So it makes me happy too
Cause you enjoy every minute, and
No one deserves it more than you.

This poem was written by Florence Binger, wife of Harvey Binger, who was the game warden in Britton for many years. It is printed with permission from their son, Ron.

How the Conservation Officers Trained the Commissioner

By Berdette Zastrow

Berdette Zastrow served on the Commission for South Dakota Game, Fish and Parks from 1987 – 1994, serving as chairperson in 1990. She was born and raised on a farm near Groton and then farmed with her husband, Bruce, at Columbia on the James River. She is an avid big game hunter and angler, and shares the tradition with four grandsons. After retiring from actively writing outdoor features for magazines and newspapers, she has written two books about her hunting adventures.

This story was published in INTERNATIONAL GAME WARDEN magazine, Winter 1993-94, near the end of Berdette's time on the commission. It is reprinted with permission from the author.

"This button runs the siren, these are the special lights, this button runs this radio and that button runs that radio. Oh yeah, here's the shotgun, remember it's a pump, and here's the .38 to put in your purse. Now remember the checklist on what to do if I get into trouble. OK, now we're set—let's go!"

While sitting in the conservation officer's pickup with a look of overwhelming confusion and terror, off we went to find some deer "shiners." And so, my "hands-on" training of "what it's like to be a conservation officer" began.

When I was first appointed to the South Dakota Game, Fish and Parks Commission, I received a phone call from my local conservation officer inviting me to lunch. It was not a division director from our head office in Pierre, it was not anyone from our regional or district office who called me, it was the conservation officer (CO).

"Lunch" turned into a three-hour presentation of just some of the philosophies, reasons behind decisions, discussions of current issues, and a lot of time spent on officer duties. Was I bored? Heck no! I found it fascinating!

What was really incredible was the fact that officers chose their profession to enhance their love of the outdoors and wildlife, not for the money. I also remember a lot of time spent discussing "privatization of wildlife." Having to deal with this issue ever since I started on the commission, I really learned to appreciate that first lecture. I soon found out that this conservation officer, and later, those in neighboring counties, were walking encyclopedias on wildlife and a ready resource for me on many issues.

At the time I was appointed, conservation officers were given the directive not to speak to commissioners, which was incomprehensible and unacceptable to me. How could commissioners get any firsthand field input? COs *are* the department, as far as the constituency is concerned. They are the ones who receive complaints, compliments, suggestions and ideas because they are "out and amongst 'em."

What better way to know what's going on out in the field than contact with these "public receptors?"

Recognizing the background in wildlife they were giving me, I took advantage and sought out their input whenever possible. Due to that fact, I acquired a great deal of respect for the wildlife law enforcement profession. Only later did I learn that they are many, many times more likely than any other law enforcement officer to be assaulted on the job.

There were some scary times when I was "riding shotgun" scouting for shiners that really drove that point home. The first night we found some illegal, beered-up characters who made the officer and me very nervous and I thought, "Now I know why I was taught all the procedures in the pickup before we left."

Later, working with an airplane giving us the location of a suspicious vehicle that had driven into a farmyard. We drove to that yard, and it was then I realized a firearm could be aimed at us out of any window in the house. It was experiences like these which really made me appreciate what our officers live with and how they lay their lives on the line, all for the protection and preservation of wildlife.

Of course, some of these early "shotgun rides" were not without humor. Working with two officers, each in their own pickup and communicating by radio, a meeting place was set in a particular area where shining had been taking place. We were stopped, called each other—in the dark, blackout lights only. In frustration, the officer I was with started the pickup, took off for another road, but then slammed on the brakes. The second officer's pickup was right in front of us! Stopping in time but somewhat shaken, we all got out and I remember the officers nervously laughing, "Boy those head-lines would've been good — *Two Game Wardens Kill Commissioner!*"

Spending time in the field with officers is extremely valuable to me. I get involved in the same situations and watch how they handle people. That is fascinating. I am always amazed how they can turn an irate, screaming, negative individual into a quiet, agreeable and sometimes pleasant little lamb, all by using their personality, with plenty of common sense and psychology.

Watching this diplomacy is a real treat. I saw this happen with a hot-headed neighbor of mine, not knowing exactly what would happen. I observed this again with another CO as a carload of irate strangers approached. That time the officer was in plain clothes and we never identified ourselves until the confrontation was over, and those peo-ple were pleased with what they had been told. Many lessons can be learned by using this quiet, positive, common-sense approach and I try to take advantage of this knowledge whenever the situation arises.

A few years ago, the commission lowered the walleye limit in the state, which was met with strong opposition from various special interest groups. A few months later, I was with an officer during a road check and it was a delight to watch how he visited with the people but still acquired all the information he needed. The situation turned out very positive and it's nice to watch our guys receive the compliments, too. I've observed relationships between COs and landowners and I was proud to have the landowners tell me they really like and respect their conservation officer.

I have lived on a farm all my life and thought I knew a lot about wildlife, their habitat, etc. Due to COs, I have received an education on wildlife and land management that rivals college classes, I'm sure. I have always respected wildlife, but never as intensely as I do now. When I was driving, I'd see wildlife here and there—nothing like the critters I can see now because I was taught how to look for them in their habitat and have fun observing them.

At the time of my appointment, I was a pheasant "flusher" only, but had grown up fishing with my father. I guess the officers saw that I needed some help in the hunting area so they went to work on me. My husband only hunted pheasants and, being as busy as he was on the farm, was happy that I would have some hunting instructors. Because of the officers, I now love hunting of all kinds and appreciate their efforts immensely. From all types of waterfowl to grouse, turkey, pheasants, whitetail and mule deer, I have enjoyed them all.

I am still receiving encouragement for two more species on my list—antelope and elk. I've been helped with fishing tips, too. When an officer recently looked into my sparse tackle box, I was quickly given a shopping list of lures, followed by lectures on fish biology. It was a CO who first talked me into hunting alone—something unheard of to me. I tried and learned a lot about myself and the wildlife I pursued. In addition to being a landowner, it's also from the COs that I learned just how bad or good some hunters' ethics are, a great concern to all of us. It was also a CO who gave me the idea for my personalized license plate: "I HUNT 2." (Other commissioners hunt and "I HUNT TOO."

Berdette Zastrow is pictured after a successful hunt.

I attend most of our regional CO meetings, seeking input from the field. It's there where I become aware of situations that I will ultimately have to handle or make a decision upon at the commission table. These meetings are where many ideas are born, where season-setting schedules start, where problems are discussed. When making commission decisions, this background information is invaluable. I don't know how an intelligent decision can be made without input from the field.

It's not only the COs in my immediate area who have advised me in the past and still continue to do so. Except new hires, I have the advantage of knowing all the COs in the state and readily seek their input if/when needed.

Commissioners have to make decisions affecting the entire state and we need information on many issues in many parts of South Dakota. I appreciate very much the working relationships I have with our COs as knowing and working with them has done a tremendous job of making my commission work easier and more meaningful with more intelligent decisions.

Working together and coordinating efforts between commissioners and COs can accomplish many goals, with the ultimate decisions being made for the good of everyone and the resource. Commissioners can help COs in their jobs, too. I never thought I'd feel proud disposing of a road kill, but I did! Coming upon a deer lying on the highway, I stopped, put on my old gloves, dragged the deer way down the ditch and removed it from the public's view. I later called the county CO and told him. To say he was surprised is putting it mildly. But why should he be called when I know what to do, am capable of doing it and can save him time and all of us money by handling it myself until he can take care of it?

I appreciate the officers' spouses, too. Like someone said, we get two employees for the price of one! Recognizing the spouses' contributions early on, I felt we should have some type of appreciation ceremony for spouses at an SDCOA convention. Yellow rose corsages were made and each spouse received an appreciation certificate from the officer along with a kiss of thanks. I obviously included my husband in the ceremony for all the wonderful family support I have received in this job. He also must answer irate phone callers, put up with weird schedules and smile sometimes even if he doesn't want to.

I have tremendously enjoyed being "trained" by the conservation officers. I feel I have received the equivalent of a degree in wildlife by now and it all has worked very well to make my decisions easier, more intelligent and more caring. One of the greatest honors I have received was the Certificate of Award from NAWEOA in Red Deer, Alberta. How pleased I was to accept that—from this international association of wildlife law enforcement professionals—the best in the world!

I know from personal experience that our conservation officers are not cold, ruthless, unfeeling cops as some perceive them to be. I have seen and felt the deep compassion they have for their fellow man and for the creatures in the wild. Yes, these officers did train me—to be more aware of my environment and to use my position to make this a better world for all of us. To each of them, I say a very grateful THANK YOU.

I'm concerned about the future of our hunting and fishing heritage. We need to have more women and children involved in our activities. I would hope that with the talented officers we have, ideas will spring forth which will help insure our youth have further involvement in the wildlife world. What else do I want? I think it would be great to have my very own badge and to be able to participate in an undercover operation. And, maybe someday, with lots of tolerance, my conservation officers will let me sing and play a song I composed for them!

Addendum: It was with the help and guidance from conservation officers which allowed me to later take South Dakota elk and antelope, for which I am forever grateful. (Added 2018)

Our Neck of the Woods: GF15-5 & GF9-5 & GF49-5

Harry Haivala grew up in Harding County, South Dakota, one of nine children. After high school, he enlisted in the Air Force. In addition to his work with South Dakota Game, Fish & Parks, Harry joined the National Guard in 1972 and retired in 1997 as a CSM(E9).

He served on the local fire department for 20 years and on the school board for six years. He was elected president of the South Dakota Peace Officers Association in 1976, as well as being elected president of the South Dakota Conservation Officers Association in 1978 and again in 1986. He received the Shikar Safari Officer of the Year award in 1987 and retired in 1993.

Harry and his wife Irene have two sons – one in Spearfish and one in Overland Park, Kansas – and five grandchildren.

For 30 years, Harry Haivala dedicated his life to working as a game warden with South Dakota Game, Fish & Parks. He started in 1964 with Arlo Hass, Ron Catlin, Bill Shattuck, Lyle Brown and Art Wren.

"It was the people I met along the way that stand out the most," said Harry. "I remember the people. Especially Jim Schroeder and Chuck Webster. They were my closest friends. Our wives were friends too."

Virgil Johnson, chief warden in the early 1960s, was the first to ask Harry about being a game warden. He was out in Buffalo sage grouse hunting and Harry was working as a butcher.

"No," said Harry in response to his question. "I think I'd like to be a highway patrolman."

Harry grew up in Buffalo, South Dakota, and returned to the area after serving in the Air Force. Shortly after his conversation with Virgil, Dave Duncan moved in next door; he was the new game warden in the area.

"It was Dave who convinced me to go to Rapid City and take the test," said Harry. The exam to work for Game, Fish & Parks included physical requirements and a certain knowledge base. It was given once a year at two or three places statewide.

"They tested you on what you knew about fish and game, as well as what you knew about South Dakota. At the time, all the wardens and biologists were hired based on that test."

Harry passed and began as a young warden in Phillip.

"My dad was sheriff of Harding County for 12 years," he said. "Before that, he was a deputy for 4 years under his brother Sam. My dad's call letters were

35-1 and when I started in Philip, mine were 31-5."

It was in these first years that he caught a break on a longtime poacher – one that officers before him had been after for years.

"It was New Year's Day," he recalls. "I was out on a lake checking ice fishermen when I spotted a car on the highway that ran by. A car I recognized."

From his spot on the ice, Harry watched the car turn off, go through a gate and up a hill.

"At the top of the hill he stopped and got a tub out of the trunk," said Harry. "He dragged it over the hill where I couldn't see what he was doing. But, when he came back, he was just carrying the tub so I knew he had thrown something out."

When the car left, Harry drove up the same hill and followed the tracks in the snow. He found a deer hide and gut pile.

"Right away I contacted our state's attorney, Robert Miller, to get a search warrant," said Harry. "He was actually on the other side of the state but, when he heard what had seen, he told me he was on his way."

Robert Miller would later become the Chief Justice of the South Dakota Supreme Court.

The local sheriff and a highway patrolman went along to serve the warrant. At the residence, they found deer on the table, mid-dinner, and more in the cellar. The rest of the deer was in the trunk of an old junk car in the yard.

"The warden in Phillip before me, Darrell Brady – he was the assistant chief warden and my boss – had followed this guy for years," said Harry. "He was very happy to hear we finally got him."

After three years in Phillip, Harry moved to Belle Fourche, where he took over for Chuck Webster. Chuck moved to Deadwood at that time and a young officer named Jim Schroeder moved into Phillip.

Before long, Schroeder would move to Sturgis, putting GF15-5 (Harry), GF9-5 (Chuck) and GF49-5 (Jim) in a neat little triangle. The trio would wreak havoc on poachers in the northern Black Hills for the remainder of their game warden careers.

"I was always a game warden," Harry said. "It seemed like if you got promoted you had to move – I liked it right where I was. Same with Jim and Chuck."

Lawrence, Meade and Butte Counties are big spaces. Harry and his neighboring officers helped each other out frequently.

"One night, I was in Chuck's area, near O'Neil pass on Highway 85," Harry recalls. "My neighbor, another Jim, had been over for dinner with his family. I was getting ready to go patrol and Jim said he would like to come along. We could do that back in the old days."

Almost to the Wyoming line, Harry saw the telltale sign of someone running a spotlight. Naturally, they went to check it out.

"We came upon a vehicle and followed it west, all blacked out. We were almost to the Wyoming line, so I decided I'd better stop them. I flipped on my lights."

It was a couple of kids… and a deer.

"They had a deer in the back, all frozen, not fresh like they'd just killed it," said Harry. "I had read in the paper earlier that evening that a deer had been stolen from a camp near O'Neil pass. The kids' story seemed to fit, so didn't think anything of it at the time. But they did get a ticket for spotlighting."

The car turned around to leave, but came back after passing Harry's truck.

"Those kids came back and told me they were going to arrest me for no tail lights!" Harry laughs.

"I was still in blackout mode. So, I flipped the switch and showed them there were lights. I advised them to move along as they were in enough trouble already. But after they drove away, I got to thinking about that newspaper article…"

Harry called the Lead Police Department and had them find and stop the vehicle so he could inspect the deer again.

"Finally, the kids admitted stealing the deer," Harry remembers. "The people they'd stolen it from said they wouldn't press charges if they could get the deer back. Dave Duncan, then the game warden in Rapid City, met me between Rapid City and Lead to escort the kids to give the deer back and apologize. But they still got the ticket for spotlighting."

Adventures in Road Checks

Back in the day, we could set up road blocks whenever we wanted. Chuck and I set one up near Rochford Road off Highway 85. It was just the two of us on the road block, so I would go farther up the road and sit in the ditch to watch people coming up.

Pickups with toppers were pretty popular back then. A truck came up with the tailgate open. A guy was sitting in the door of the topper with a deer on the tailgate, trying to get the old metal tag locked on the deer.

He couldn't see me yet, so I ran up and grabbed a hold of the deer leg and tag. We proceeded up the road and he had to show Chuck an untagged deer!

Ticket given…

How many gizzards does it take…?

Another time we were doing a road check in the lower part of Spearfish Canyon. Chuck stayed with the vehicle and I went up a ways and hid out in the ditch.

I saw a vehicle go by and then noticed turkey innards scattered along the road.

"Hey Chuck!" I yelled, "how many gizzards does a turkey have?"

"ONE!" came the reply.

"Well it looks like this one had THREE!"

They guy who had dumped them finally admitted he had too many turkeys.

Ticket given...

By Land and by Air

Late one night I happened upon some coon hunters using spotlights. I snuck up on them, but when I flipped on my lights and siren, they jackrabbited!

I gave chase and radioed Jim and Chuck for assistance. The perpetrators were throwing out coons along the way, even a gun! I continued on the radio to tell the boys where to pick these things up for evidence.

We went 26 miles before they finally gave up in Newell. It was a wild ride!

I had another wild ride after coon hunters a different time. I radioed the town cop for help to block the road.

"To heck with you!" he told me. "The state buys your car, but I have to buy my own!"

But a highway patrolman answered the call and finally got the guilty party rounded up in a pasture. By the time I arrived, he already had them cuffed!

Sometimes, we were able to take the plane up to look for spotlights. One particular time I was in the air, while Jim and Chuck were on the ground. I had a guy in my sights, and they finally caught up to him on the ground. When they had him stopped, I asked the pilot to swoop down over them – had to say hi and let him know how he got caught!

It wasn't always us who had the plane up, though. I once got a call for assistance from the officer in Buffalo. He had a guy using a plane for hunting coyotes and fox without a permit.

When he came in to land, he had no lights – we heard the plane coming but couldn't see it. When he taxied up to the hangar, we were waiting for him. He had a bunch of carcasses tied to the struts of the plane. Turned out it was a cousin of mine! But we made the arrest...

Something to Grouse About

Near Belle Fourche is the geographical center of the nation. Now, the marker is moved into town, but it used to be outside of town in a fenced-off area.

Cars often parked there, so during grouse and antelope season I would sit there and stop cars that had guns or otherwise appeared to be hunting.

Sharp tail grouse vexed a great many people.

At that spot, I arrested a former game warden because he had sharp tail grouse instead of sage grouse.

"How do you tell the difference?!" he asked me.

"Well," I said, "you tell me. You were the game warden."

Another time I visited with the principal of a Rapid City school during the sage grouse season. He was stopped at a little country store northeast of Newell.

"Have you been hunting?" I asked him.

"Why yes!" he replied. "I've got some fine grouse in my car."

Indeed, he did – sharp tail grouse, not sage. I gave him the news.

"How do you tell the difference?!" he asked.

"Well sir, it's a matter of education," I told him.

Fish Tales

Early one morning while checking fishermen on the inlet canal at Orman Dam, I came upon a lady fishing whom I had known for a long time. We conversed for a while.

"Well, I suppose you want to see my thing," she said.

"Yes," I replied. "Then I will look at your fishing license."

One winter day, I was checking ice fisherman at Newell Lake by snowmobile. I came upon an ice house. When the fishermen saw that I was a game warden, he entered his house and came right back out again.

I checked his license and then his legal limit of lines. Curious, I went inside the house to look around. Down an ice hole, I could see a line dangling with nothing on it, and on the lake bottom a coiled line with a minnow swimming around.

The individual finally admitted he had cut the extra line when he ducked into the house when he saw who I was. Ticket given…

Marriage on Ice

By Owen Meadows

Owen began his career with South Dakota Game, Fish & Parks working for the Parks Division in Watertown, where he grew up. After becoming a state game warden, he was stationed in Hot Springs where he served from 1967-2000. Owen was a founding member of the South Dakota Conservation Officers Association (SDCOA) and also served on the board in various capacities.

In the mid-1960s, prior to being hired as a game warden, I worked with the parks division in Watertown. Everybody with Game, Fish & Parks (GFP) was out of the same location, the same building in Watertown where I grew up. It's the same building today!

Because we worked out of the same building, Harold Lunde, the game warden, and I got to know each other a bit.

"I kinda think you might like my line of work," he said to me one day. "Why don't you ride with me a bit and see if you do."

So I rode with him. The rest is history. I was hired as a state game warden in October 1967. If it hadn't been for Harold, I don't think I would have picked up on the idea of being a game warden; I credit Harold Lunde for my career in wildlife law enforcement.

Before I was off to my own station in Hot Springs, I was out patrolling with Harold one day. We were out looking for ice fishermen around Watertown. We drove to an access spot on Lake Pelican. It had snowed about an inch overnight and you could see one set of tracks driving out there. The track made a circle and a guy was out there fishing.

We could see he had more than two lines and, at that time, you were only allowed two. Well, he had four. So we drove out there; Harold checked his license and asked who else was there.

"Oh, my wife!" he said. "My wife. I don't know… she must be around here someplace. I think she went over there."

He pointed across the lake.

It wasn't very far to the next bank. Maybe a quarter mile.

"I think she went over there," he said again. "She had to go to the bathroom."

There was fresh snow on the ground… and no people tracks.

There were no tracks at all going the direction he said she had gone.

So Harold quizzed him a little bit and then the fisherman started walking around his vehicle. He appeared to be searching for the wife he swore was with him. He looked under the car; he opened all four doors in search of his elusive wife. Harold followed him while he looked in the back seat, then in the front. The fisherman even picked up the floor mats to see if she might be hiding underneath.

"I don't know," the guy says again, completing his search and looking at Harold.

"Well, you've got too many lines out," said Harold. "I'm going to give you a summons for too many lines."

So, went through the process – signed him up, told him his court date and everything else he needed to know.

And as we were parting company, the last thing this fella had to say was, "boy, is my wife gonna catch hell when I get home!"

A Hunter vs. a Sportsman

Harold Lunde began his career with Game, Fish & Parks in the early 1960s. He was stationed in Hosmer and Watertown. In 1972, he relocated to Rapid City where he worked as the regional supervisor. In 1973, he became the Custer State Park Assistant Superintendent. Harold retired in 1977. Though he passed away in 2015, Owen Meadows credits Lunde for steering him toward a career as a Game Warden. This story is told by Owen Meadows.

It was opening day of pheasant season in 1972. Harold Lunde was down from the Rapid City office in Fall River County to assist me. It may seem odd that help would be necessary in this area, a county so far from the prime pheasant regions in South Dakota. However, part of eastern Fall River County is irrigated farm land and hosts a pheasant population comparable to areas like Chamberlain or Winner.

Unlike most seasons, when shooting hours begin pre-sunrise, pheasant season allows for a leisurely breakfast. That is what Harold and I were enjoying when a hunter stopped at our booth.

He shoved his license at Harold.

"I want my license checked *now* so you don't bother me while I am out hunting," he demanded. Without a word, Harold took the license and placed it in his shirt pocket. He continued to eat.

The hunter repeated, "I want my license checked now. What's the deal?"

"As soon as we are finished with breakfast, I will look at your license," Harold replied coolly. "Until then, don't bother us."

The hunter unhappily stood at the far side of the restaurant until we finished our leisurely breakfast.

This man is correctly defined as a hunter and not a sportsman.

It's a Wonder Nobody Ever Tried to Shoot Us

Arlo Haase began his career with South Dakota Game, Fish & Parks in 1964. After a couple years at his first station in Plankinton he transferred to Milbank and spent the rest of his 36-year career in the northeast corner of the state.

Dave Wicks began his rookie year in August 1972 with Arlo to guide him. He spent about a year and a half in Sisseton and Roberts County. He moved to Watertown in 1974 and in 1978 became the assistant regional supervisor for law enforcement. Dave retired in 2009.

"The best part?" Dave Wicks twists the napkin in his hands, still large and strong in retirement. "Making sure my guys went home every night. That was the best part of my job."

Wicks, who retired as the assistant regional supervisor for law enforcement, retired, sits at his kitchen table next to Arlo Haase, longtime coworker and friend.

Arlo grins, light in his eyes as he remembers his work as a conservation officer in the northeast corner of South Dakota.

"I just had so dang much fun," he says with a laugh. Even now, mischief and joy outshine his age, especially talking about his job. Health issues forced Arlo to retire in 2000.

"I became a conservation officer right out of college," he said. Arlo graduated from South Dakota State University with a Wildlife and Fisheries Sciences degree. "I never took any other job or promotion in the department. I started out in Plankinton, but took an opening in the northeast as soon as I could get it. Judy, my wife, and I really wanted to get back to the northeast, closer to where we grew up in Day County."

After a brief time in Sisseton, Arlo spent the majority of his career in Milbank. August 1, 1972, Dave Wicks came on the force and was stationed in Sisseton, Arlo's old territory.

"Arlo was my training officer," said Dave. "I really learned a lot from him. We had a lot of gill netting in our area, especially on Lake Traverse and Big Stone Lake, which are both on the Minnesota border. We worked with Minnesota officers frequently – they would watch our side and we would watch theirs. We would sit up on high hills and wait for lights along the shore at night."

Gill net action was especially lively in the spring, after ice-out but before the fishing season opened in Minnesota. Of course, gill nets are only legal in extremely specific circumstances.

One chilly spring night during Dave's rookie years, Arlo had a tip on a gill net location.

"Nobody lives along here," Arlo had told Dave about the cabin they were staked out near. "There won't be anybody around."

They separated. Arlo went down the beach a ways, but the only way for Dave to see the shore from his location was to climb a tree.

"So I spent the night in that tree," Dave laughs, recalling the memory. "There I was, watching this dock where this net was supposed to be and waiting. Come morning, I felt … funny. I started looking around and here's this woman standing in the window where nobody was supposed to be home. And there I was right in front of her … up in the tree!"

"It had snowed overnight!" Arlo remembers. "It snowed all night long, so it was all over, except for Dave's clothes. There he was, everything covered in snow but him!"

"And we had those bright red coats then!" said Dave. "This lady was looking right at me, but she didn't have her glasses on. She had just gotten out of bed, because it was just sun up. I tried not to move, but I sure didn't want to get shot for peeking in somebody's window! When she left the room, I got the hell out of that tree!"

Next thing Dave knew, Arlo was yelling that someone was at the net.

"That woman never did see me. I could have been shot as a window peeker!" Dave exclaims, still indignant after all these years. "But we caught the bad guys and I didn't get shot out of the tree. I know at the age I am now (72), if I had to sit in a tree all night, I wouldn't be able to get down! I'd be so stiff, ka-boom, I'd have to fall out to get back on the ground!"

"You were the rookie," Arlo reminds him with a smirk. "I had been on a while, so you know who got to sit in the tree. I changed my system after he became my supervisor."

If they didn't have enough information to watch a particular dock, they had another technique for working gill netters.

"We would take a small boat that didn't make much noise," said Dave. "We would drag a hook along the shore until we found a gill net in the water. Then we would sit on it until they came to take the fish out, usually about sunrise. So we had to spend the night there, hiding in the woods."

"One night," remembers Arlo, "we were on a gill net waiting for them to come out of the cabin to pull it up. I was tiptoeing along the shore line, getting closer to the guys, and finally I turned my flashlight on. The guy pulling in the nets says 'Ya dumb shit, shut that light out!'

He was pretty surprised to see a game warden and not one of his buddies! It's a wonder nobody ever tried to shoot us."

The practice of using gill nets often led to folks being over the possession limit on fish. Arlo and Dave had one case they had been working for quite a while before they had enough evidence for a search warrant.

"When we decided to raid, they locked the doors and wouldn't come out," recalls Arlo. "We had a sheriff and a couple conservation officers (COs) from Minnesota with us. All of the sudden, you could hear the toilets flushing in the house… they actually started flushing the fish."

"They didn't want to get caught," said Dave. "They had quite a bunch of fish. We already had the goods on 'em, they just went through a lot of trouble. I think they might've plugged their sewer up…"

"We even found fish in the beds where their kids were sleeping," said Arlo, chuckling. "There was a lot of fun and a lot of interesting times along with the job."

Gill nets were only part of the work Haase and Wicks did together.

There were deer cases and even an instance of a man shooting an eagle.

"This guy used to drive around the country in his pickup shooting at what he thought were chicken hawks," said Dave. "One particular time, he shot the biggest damn chicken hawk he'd ever seen. Turned out it was an eagle."

"A neighbor turned him in," said Arlo. "He got a fine and they confiscated the truck, which I think the feds used for an undercover rig."

"Remember my first bust as a rookie, out south of Rosholt?" asks Dave.

"Yeah, I remember," said Arlo with a gleam in his eye.

The pair were watching four guys in a field from a high spot on a hill. Geese were dropping, but the group kept shooting. Finally, one of the vehicles came out, so Arlo and Dave stopped them and checked things out.

They had their exact limit.

"I think the other guys still have a couple to go down there, but we got our limit and we're going home," the hunter told them.

"So we went down to talk to the guys who were still in the field," said Dave. "Before we got there, they shot about four more and the geese were all scattered around. They were clearly over their limit of one Canada goose per person."

"If we walk around here and find them," Arlo told the men, "it will be worse on you than if you show us."

"They wouldn't," said Dave. "So, we walked around a bit and found the geese, along with more stashed in a combine sitting nearby."

One member of the incriminated hunting party was the president of the local sportsmen's club, a business owner and a general big shot in the community.

"What am I supposed to say!??!" he fumed at Arlo and Dave.

Arlo, however, had enough of the whole situation.

"Tell the judge your wife has two assholes and you're one of 'em," Arlo shot back at the angry hunter.

Dave's eyes widen, recalling his shock at the time. "Here I am on my first big rookie bust and Arlo comes up with *that* little gem. Oohhh my, I thought. But we made it through."

"They were five or six over their limit," said Arlo. "This was back when you could only have one Canada goose. South Dakota Game, Fish & Parks was trying to get them reestablished in the area."

"I remember using snowmobiles and car hoods to drag bales out to fields for geese to use for nesting," said Dave. "That effort was probably the most successful program the department ever did in terms of reestablishing something. Now, there are geese everywhere!"

The "Breast" Exam

By Ron Catlin

Ron Catlin grew up in Platte, S.D. He graduated from South Dakota State University in 1964 and began work in Vermillion as a state game warden that same summer. Ron was the game warden (conservation officer) in Vermillion until 1972 when he transferred to Yankton in the same capacity.

In 1978, Ron accepted the position of Law Enforcement Staff Specialist or Chief of Law Enforcement in Pierre, when the department went through a re-organization. Ron held that position until his retirement in the fall of 1999.

During those years in Pierre, Ron continued to hold his law enforcement certification and to work law enforcement in the field as an administrator in the law area.

After his retirement, Ron filled in as a conservation officer for two fall seasons in Hughes, Stanley and Sully counties. He got to go "back to his roots as a field officer" for a couple of years before totally hanging it up.

Ron continues to live in Pierre after losing his wife, Marrietta in June 2018, after a courageous two-year battle with breast cancer. Also in Pierre are Ron's son Joel, wife Kristi and two granddaughters, Olivia and Addison. Another son, Stephen, lives in Virginia along with three grandchildren, Zachary, Tyler and Stephanie.

Every fall brings with it another series of hunting seasons from the dove season in early September through the waterfowl season ending in February. Some are similar from year to year and sometimes certain events stand out in your mind and stay in your memory for years afterwards.

One such event began with a phone call from Howard Lovrien in early November of 1976. Howard was a Special Agent with the U.S. Fish and Wildlife Service, or a Federal Game Warden as they were more commonly called, who was stationed in Aberdeen.

This was a phone call I welcomed and looked forward to most years when fall rolled around. It was an invite to come over to Running Water for a couple of days and work the duck season on the river. Howard had purchased an old cabin on the banks of the Missouri River several miles west of Springfield, S.D. in a very small community known as Running Water.

In earlier times a ferry boat operated out of Running Water, hauling people and vehicles across the river to Nebraska – there were no bridges across the river on this stretch of the Missouri River. The nearest bridge was at Yankton, about 30 miles downstream to the east, or Pickstown which was almost as far west at Fort Randall Dam.

This stretch of the Missouri River from just below the town of Springfield to Running Water contained some of the finest areas in the state for waterfowl hunting. Siltation from the Niobrara River coming out of Nebraska had turned the area into miles of cattails, sand bars and shallow waterways, providing a haven for waterfowl and almost endless opportunities for duck hunters. Waterfowl hunters primarily from South Dakota, Nebraska and Iowa keyed in on this area each fall to pursue their sport.

I was the conservation officer at Yankton at the time and looked forward to running over to Bon Homme County, my neighboring county to the west. We arranged to meet at Howard's cabin the following afternoon to plan for the next day. Upon my arrival I was met by not only Howard, but Special Agent David Fisher from Pierre and Leroy Sorenson, the local conservation officer assigned to Bon Homme County from Tyndall.

Howard's cabin was truly a "man cave." To say it was rustic was an understatement, though it did have electricity. A two-hole outdoor toilet behind the house made it especially memorable for those few of us who actually lived in a period of our youth where outdoor outhouses and Sears-Roebuck catalogs were how things were.

Howard's outhouse, however, was quite luxurious – it had real toilet paper! And, it was customized: one hole was quite a bit larger than the other and had a sign over it, saying that side was "for wide-assed biologists." It also had a roll of paper towels to go with the "wide" theme, further ribbing our game biologist counterparts, whom we in law enforcement liked to hassle from time to time.

The cabin also accommodated its own wildlife populations in the form of mice, bats, spiders and assorted varieties of insects. It was a nice, well-rounded mix of critters.

Howard was also the chief cook in his kitchen over the old cook stove. The smells of bacon frying, eggs, pancakes and other goodies made the cabin seem like a 5-star restaurant. Roast duck was common evening table fare when we were lucky enough to bag a few ducks the previous day while mingling in plain clothes with the other duck hunters on the river, whom we were observing and monitoring as part of our warden duties. And a regular side dish to any of Howard's meals was dumplings. I've never been a big fan of dumplings, but we all ate Howard's dumplings and at least pretended to enjoy them. We always had an assortment of beverages for after supper, but a staple with Howard was a jug of Rhine wine. Seemed to go well with duck! And most anything else, for that matter.

Howard was always the first one up at o-dark-thirty to get breakfast started. About the time the bacon was frying, Howard would do the "wake-up" call which was a very loud series of mallard "high-ball" calls, usually used to attract distant flocks of ducks. This definitely roused a person from even the deepest sleep.

With breakfast out of the way, we loaded up our boats with decoys, warm weather gear, shotguns, duck calls, lunch and other gear needed for a day on the river.

On this day, I accompanied Howard in his Grumman sportcraft. Dave and Leroy were in the other boat, working a different part of the river that day.

As the eastern sky was starting to lighten, we started down the river. We meandered through the various waterways trying to find the location we had picked to set up our spread where we could observe other groups of hunters. This was a pretty nice day considering it was November – about 30 degrees, partly cloudy and not much wind. With the small canoe-like Grumman sportcraft, we did not need a big wind.

We finally arrived at what looked like the general area we wanted; there was a cluster of cattails to conceal the boat and shallow enough water to toss out a couple dozen duck decoys. We had some open water areas to our south and west and pretty good flowing water through cattails to the south.

The cattails were high enough to conceal the boat and still low enough to stand and see what was happening around us. Amazingly, we heard no shots before legal shooting time on this morning. Too often, shots are heard well before legal shooting hours and it is extremely difficult to locate these early shooters and issue the tickets they deserve. There is such a small window of opportunity to locate these hunters in the semi-darkness, identify who shot, and get to them before legal shooting time.

Fortunately, on this morning we did not have that problem. This was during the time frame that South Dakota and most central flyway states were in the point system of determining duck limits. Different species of ducks were awarded point values. Your limit was reached when your last duck shot reached or exceeded 100 points.

Basically, redheads and canvasbacks had a point value of 100. Hen mallards were 70 points and most other ducks, including drake mallards, were 20 points each. It was almost sunrise before the first ducks began to mill around. Howard hailed in a small flock of mallards shortly after sunrise and we managed to shoot two greenheads. Things were quiet for a while before we heard quite a volley of shots from about a half mile directly upriver, west of our location. We could see ducks flare up from that distance, but could not tell what was actually being taken.

About every ten minutes thereafter we were hearing more shots from that direction. It appeared to be the only active duck blind being hunted that day. Each volley was about a dozen or more shots so we assumed this party to be probably at least four hunters, possibly a couple more. They had an excellent location and apparently had a very good spread of decoys as the birds were really keying in on their spread. There would be some lulls in the action, but then another volley and birds would flare up in the distance.

About an hour and a half after the shooting began, we noticed a duck floating by in the current about 50 yards south of us. It appeared to be a hen mallard. A few minutes later two more hen mallards appeared floating down the river.

Now it had our attention. We pulled our boat out of the rushes and motored over and picked up the two ducks. They were hen mallards and the breasts had been removed.

We made a run downstream and caught up with the first duck we saw. It also was a hen mallard with the breasts removed. Now we had a mission.

How many other hen mallards had met this fate? We had found three and there were probably more. We waited about another hour, still hearing shooting from that general location with some regularity. We decided we had better get up there and see if we could locate that group of hunters before they left for the day.

Upstream about a half mile, we saw a well-concealed setup with two jon boats, end to end, pulled into the rushes and a large spread of decoys. This should be the group we heard doing the shooting.

As we pulled up to the blind, we identified ourselves as state and federal game wardens and that we would like to check their birds and licenses. There were six hunters in full hunting gear, complete with chest waders standing in the two twenty-foot-long, flat-bottomed jon boats. There was a full wrap-around commercial blind covering the full length of the two boats, making it look like cattails.

The hunters were from Iowa and hunting on non-resident Nebraska hunting licenses, which was allowed on these boundary waters between South Dakota and Nebraska.

Inside, we found a large assortment of coolers, decoy bags, clothing, food containers, gun cases and other gear. Howard announced that he would be checking hunting licenses and shotguns for plugs and I would be checking their ducks.

Howard stayed outside the boats checking licenses while I climbed inside the blind with the hunters. On the front deck of the boat they had 28 greenhead mallard drakes neatly laid out in two rows. The hunters advised us they shot only mallard drakes as they were concerned for the welfare of the mallard population and were only doing the right thing by not shooting hens.

We certainly expected otherwise, so I let them know we'd like to check their boats for any other ducks and check their boat safety equipment, such as life preservers. They said to help ourselves and continued to visit with Howard as I went through the two boats on my hands and knees.

These were very tight quarters with three large duck hunters in each boat and lots of gear in a small space. I went through all the coolers, some with food, others with drinks, and into every crevice I could find in each boat. Howard also looked around the outside of the boats. I then worked my way back through the boats, having to brush against each hunter as I tried to get around each one of them in the narrow opening at the top of the blind.

Going by the third hunter, I detected some kind of abnormality at his midsection. At this moment, I told the hunters I was going to do a "breast exam" and reached into the waders of the rather large duck hunter I had just passed by.

Lo and behold, I discovered a bread bag with eight duck breasts inside. The hunters' faces suddenly changed from jovial to the tell-tale "oh crap!"

Two of the hunters were issued federal tickets for exceeding the daily bag of waterfowl and possession of waterfowl without plumage (the bag of duck breasts).

Far from being "concerned sportsmen" worried about saving ducks, they were shooting their share of hens also, putting the greenheads on their pile and breasting out the hens and throwing the carcasses back into the river to float away.

They were also doing some filming of their hunt. Nice guys!

All in all, it was a very good morning's work for us. As we finished all the bookwork and pulled away from the blind with the bag of duck breasts and the mallard drakes we had seized as evidence of the violations, I still can hear Howard saying "I can't believe you actually went down into that guy's waders and found those duck breasts!"

But I did, I found the missing breasts and no one contested that I had done so.

Several years later, for Howard's retirement from the U.S. Fish and Wildlife Service, I wrote my first poem, or Ode as I called it, as a remembrance of the good times I and other wardens had over the years with Howard. The Ode was read at his party and many in attendance could relate

Unfortunately, a few short years later Howard passed away as a result of brain cancer at a relatively young age. He was a great guy, a great officer, and will long be remembered by those who knew him.

ODE (OWED) TO HOWARD LOVRIEN

I tried to remember the good things you did and dwell on your positive side,

But each thought of a positive action was offset by the pranks that you've tried.

I remember your training of Louie in the handling of minority rights;

His interrogation of Cleveland brought you many delights.

I remember awaking from a deep, deep sleep

By a ringing phone and a voice real deep.

It said "this is Special Investigator Smith from A T & F

And if you ain't worried now you must be deaf!"

"You've been making home brew and selling it too,

We've got our sources, now what about you?"

"Your license, boy, is it current and paid?

And the quantities, fellow, how much have you made?"

I remember I squirmed, oh how I did squirm.

Who knows if you're right when the Feds are concerned!

He questioned my ethics- "An alcoholic are you?"
I blurted "My no! I hardly touch any brew!"
After baring my soul for ten minutes or so,
Being prodded, exploited and forced to eat crow,
He finally got down to "When was your last drink?"
I quickly responded without time to think.
"Oh, at least 3 weeks since I've touched a drop!"
He answered right back, "you lie well for a cop!"
"I know that last Wednesday some Feds were in town
And some jugs of your wine to their room you took down."
The plot having thickened way beyond fret,
I fumbled for words and broke out in a sweat.
As I sat there and trembled in frustration and fear,
The voice on the phone says "Hi! Lovrien here!"

Many miles have passed and some time has passed too
Since Howard pulled off that despicable coo.
With Howard transferred and suspicions relaxed,
A call is received from a lawyer for facts.
A big eastern lawyer from a prominent firm
With some legal baloney to cause me to squirm.
His client whose rights have been shattered and torn,
Will cause me to wish I'd never been born.
His facts are complete, with names I know too.
His points are well taken, he's wanting to sue.
I thought I'd done well with that wild goose raiser,
but all of my reasons did not even phase her.
"Her hubby has served his time in jail

so your denial's unfounded- get off your tail!"
After minutes of alibies, hedging and worry,
Of subjecting myself to his threats and his fury,
the announcement is made and my face turns red,
Howard Lovrien here—What else can be said.

There were times at the cabin, the ducks cooked in wine,
The frog legs, the mushrooms and thrips were all fine.
With the ducks flying high and temperature cold,
Howard's 'high-baller' call brought ducks to the fold.
"Here come the ducks—get down and freeze!"
Where's Howard? In the decoys, waders down at his knees.
Anyone knows who's spent time in the blind,
That Rhine wine and coffee cause kidneys to bind.

Of hunting dogs Howard has memories galore.
Most of them bad, he's all but lost score.
A U.S. attorney had a dandy it seems,
dumb, senseless and ignorant, whatever that means.

I remember a hunt with some Feds after dawn,
When three suzies floated by with their breasts neatly gone.
Howard and I in his neat little Grumman,
Roared up the river from where they were comin'.
There were the culprits, Iowaegions they were,
With 28 mallards, all drakes to be sure.
Each boat was searched, each cranny and crack,
Nothing was found from the front to the back.

Our suspicion aroused, they couldn't be straight,
A breast search was conducted and one man had eight!
The tickets were written, the evidence secured,
And a lecture from Agent Lovrien was heard.
On the evils of poaching and the filming they'd done,
"A lousy example to your friends and your son.
Your films will preserve this memorable day.
Did you get shots of the hens which were drifting away?"

I'll remember those good times, the pinches we made,
Those times spent together I never would trade.
I'll remember those set-ups you pulled off, you stinker!
The ones that I swallowed hook, line and sinker.
I'm glad that you'll be here for years many more
Cause I owe you so many to even the score.
So enjoy your retirement, your family and friends,
long hours by the river, the relaxation it lends.
But beware of the phone calls that you will still get,
Cause I've got all those years to settle the debt!
Good luck, Howard!!

In Hot Pursuit

Dave Gray began his career with South Dakota Game, Fish & Parks in 1968. He was stationed in Phillip, Custer and Huron before returning to the Black Hills in the late 1990's, where he finished his career as the Law Enforcement Supervisor.

As told by Owen Meadows, this story recaps an eventful evening in early December 1975. Dave Gray, who passed away in February 2017, had received a tip about plans to poach a buffalo in Wind Cave National Park. Dave called Owen, his neighboring officer, to assist.

"There was a time when you could work every night of the year," begins Owen. "We kinda did, I guess. This is a story I was involved with because I provided backup the night of the incident."

Dave called Owen and said he had information about some guys planning to kill a buffalo in Wind Cave National Park. His informant knew the crime was going to be on this certain evening. When the night arrived, Dave was in Wind Cave. He was staked out on the inside of a tall fence for elk and buffalo.

"I was up in Custer State Park, not very far away," said Owen. "A couple miles, maybe. It wasn't too long before Dave gave me a little shout on the radio – somebody was coming down the road.

He let them go by and then he heard a couple shots. Of course, it was going to take them a while to load this critter. So, he trotted over to the gate and blocked that road. He threw the chain around it and just waited for them to leave. Figured he had them corralled."

Owen maintained his position, accompanied by a deputy sheriff from Fall River County. They waited to hear from Dave.

"Well, those boys got their critter loaded up and started heading west again, back from where they came," Owen says, laughing. "Apparently they didn't even stop or slow down. They saw this gate in front of them and just gave 'er the gas. The chain that held the two swinging gates together just popped and away they went."

Dave Gray was right behind them, in hot pursuit.

"In the meantime," said Owen, "I was taking my time to get around in front of them. Dave gets on the radio and says 'they just drove through the gate, broke it open!' We didn't figure they would get through the gate. Well, they did.

So Dave was right on their tail, red lights flashing. I still had a pretty good chunk of country to cover to get around to where they were, so I wasn't right behind him. The chase went on 2 or 3 miles in Wind Cave, then they peeled off and went onto a forest service trail.

But Dave Gray was right behind them! Right on them. And he could see there were three guys in the vehicle. With his spotlight and head-lights, he was pretty much able to identify them. Anyway, they drove in the woods for maybe two miles, up to the top of a hill and they bailed. All three of them jumped out of the pickup."

So there was Dave Gray with three guys in the woods and a pickup with a dead buffalo in it.

"Dave was telling me all this on the radio," continues Owen. "I got there about 5 or 10 minutes after they bailed out. We had the vehicle and Dave had an idea of who they were. We called the wrecker and had the pickup and the buffalo hauled back to Custer. Dave confis-cated the firearms and spotlight and other stuff they had left behind."

It only took a day to find them. With the help of the Sheriff's Office in Custer, the trio was rounded up the following day.

"Of course, they denied it," recalls Owen. "But anyway, it was kind of a wild chase."

Little did Dave and Owen know, they would soon find out just how wild it could have been.

"Later," recalls Owen, "Dave found out the guy in the middle, who was pretty notorious… they all were… but this guy was flat out a criminal. He was more than a poacher, he was a burglar and everything else. Anyway, he was in the middle and the two others had quite a time talking him into NOT shooting at Dave while they were making their getaway. He was kind of a sitting duck behind them with his headlights, a spotlight and red lights going. Dave got lucky there. If it hadn't been for these guys talking the third guy out of shooting at the patrol pickup, who knows…"

The three men were convicted of killing a buffalo in Wind Cave National Park, which meant there were state and federal charges. Owen recalls they were also charged with eluding an officer.

"Sometimes you get this information and it doesn't pan out," said Owen. "But this panned out really well because the day, time and location were right. This was a good case, made with the help of a tip from someone who didn't want this to happen to our wildlife resources. Also, nobody got shot."

The Brotherhood of Wildlife Law Enforcement

By Chuck Atkins

Chuck Atkins grew up on a farm near Tea, South Dakota. He graduated from Lennox High School and received a bachelor's degree in Sociology from Dakota Wesleyan University in Mitchell. As a state game warden, he was stationed in Lemmon and Salem. Later, he served as assistant regional supervisor in Chamberlain. After six years with South Dakota Game, Fish & Parks, he and his wife owned and operated a dairy farm near Tea, South Dakota. In 1984 they sold the farm. Chuck went to work for the USDA and spent almost 20 years as a district director for the Farm Service Agency in Rapid City. Chuck and Jan, his wife of 51 years, retired in 2007 and moved to Lake Oahe north of Pierre where they golf and fish, and Chuck hunts.

"It seems like yesterday, but it was long ago," just like Bob Seger said in "Against the Wind."

1968 was 50 years ago; it is not easy to recall the time we were living in. On April 4th of that year, Dr. Martin Luther King, Jr. was shot and killed. Robert Kennedy, who had just won the California and South Dakota democratic primaries on May 4th, was shot and killed May 5th by a 24-year-old Jordanian, Sirhan Sirhan. We had over 500,000 troops deployed to South Vietnam. Times were tense, to say the least. Nixon was elected that November.

There were five of us hired as South Dakota State Game Wardens on July 1st of that year – Jack Hantz, Bob Walton, Dave Gray, Lee Vanderbush and me.

Chief Game Warden C.B. Gunderson conducted the swearing-in ceremony in Sioux Falls after we completed our training.

A few days later in Pierre, "Gundy" as he was known, led us toward the closet in his office. There, he literally dragged a wooden apple crate out of a closet… it was full of rusty US Navy .38 caliber revolvers.

They had no grips and looked like rusty skeletons dredged up from the Missouri River. Mine had a grommet on the bottom of the handle with a length of rawhide still hanging on.

Gundy said, "A little steel wool and a bluing job and they will be good as new."

That proved not to be true. On the practice range, about as much shrapnel came out the sides as it did the barrel!

But it mattered not – we were all elated to get these jobs that every red-blooded young man (now we can say, thankfully, "person") in South Dakota aspired to. We were the guardians of the Midwest traditions of hunting and fishing.

A very exciting – but shocking – first day

On our first week of training, Lee Vanderbush and I were sent down to Yankton to work with wardens Floyd Gaarder and Bill Shattuck. We would work boaters and fishermen on the Missouri River above Yankton.

It was the 4th of July, hot and sultry. We had just launched the boat when we got a call about a drowning on the James River just east of Yankton. We quickly loaded the boat back on the trailer and were soon heading down the highway, siren blaring and lights ablaze. We were going so fast, the boat literally jumped off the trailer at the railroad tracks and at every other rise in the road, pushed up by the summer heat.

When we reached the river, we found the scene to be a family reunion, very large. More than 200 people lined the trail down to the river. They were yelling and waving their hands and shaking their fists as we backed down to get the boat in the water.

They were understandably upset. Two of their family members, teenagers, had disappeared while swimming in the murky water.

When they started pounding on the hood of the car, Floyd jumped out and literally threw one of the hood pounders into the crowd by the seat of his pants. That set the tone for the rest – they gave us some clearance and kept quiet.

Later, the two bodies were recovered. As we left the scene, the crowd was still angry. I remember Bill saying "Well boys, you better get used to it. The public demands a lot and rarely says thanks."

The events of that day had a tremendous impact on me as a rookie on my first day of work. It's one I will never forget and one that most people aspiring to become a game warden never hear about, think about or even expect to be involved in.

In the face of all this, we remained passionate about the job we did, determined to keep doing it, and tried to do it better every chance we got.

An Idea Begins to Take Shape

A few years after I started, Game Warden Owen Meadows of Hot Springs went to meet with the State Game and Fish Commission in an attempt to discuss starting a conservation officers association. To my knowledge, that was the first mention of an association for game wardens in South Dakota.

After four or five years working as a South Dakota Conservation Officer, the need for some professional changes became obvious.

One change which was critical and undermined our work was the fact that we were not "peace officers" in South Dakota. That meant if we came upon a violation related to something other than GFP or wildlife laws, we would have to make a citizen's arrest. We were legally on our own in that case. We also had no false arrest insurance – a huge liability.

In 1971 Dick Kneip was elected Governor of South Dakota. At the time, I was the game warden in Salem, which was Kneip's home town. With the help and encouragement of my neighboring officers, especially Dan Plut of Freeman and Harris Sundling of Canton, I took advantage of the hometown connection and sent a letter to the South Dakota State Game Fish & Parks Commission. I asked for a chance to meet with them and they consented.

When I told them why I was there, which was to get their support for a state conservation officers association, they asked why we thought we needed one. That was the easy part. "To better the profession," I said.

"As long as you are not in here every year arguing for a raise," they responded, "we'll support the association."

That was really all the encouragement we needed. At our first meeting held in Fort Thompson, as I recall, about half the game wardens in the state attended. We voted in favor of forming an association and nearly everyone signed up as charter members at our first meeting. We elected Floyd Gaarder president. Ron Catlin was elected secretary and the rest is history.

After a few years, we got newly issued sidearms, false arrest insurance, peace officer status including retirement, and new badges and uniforms. Later on, our yearly wages were almost doubled.

It may not seem like much now, but at the time I was hired, we qualified for food stamps and it took a degree to get the job.

It is important to remember that the South Dakota Conservation Officers Association (SDCOA) was born out of a need for many professional improvements. The world was changing. The world of law enforcement was changing. We had to be part of it.

Events like the Supreme Court decision that gave way to what we now know as Miranda rights or the Miranda warning forever changed the way law enforcement officers detained and questioned suspects.

Even more importantly, the SDCOA came about through the will and hard work of almost every game warden in the state at the time, and their passion for their work. It has taken even more hard work to keep the association going throughout the years.

But, even as officers have come and gone, the passion for the work has remained. And they keep trying to do it better every chance they get.

Hey Texaco Man!

A lot has changed over the years, especially where uniforms are concerned.

If you want to see what a State Game Warden looked like in 1968, Google 'That Texaco Man.' You had to be really careful around gas stations – several times people walked up to me and said "fill 'er up and check the oil…"

Helping People Love the Outdoors

Tom LeFaive began his career with South Dakota Game, Fish & Parks in 1973 as a game warden. He started his training in Watertown and was stationed in Aberdeen. After a few years in northeastern South Dakota he moved west, accepting a position as deputy director of Custer State Park. In 1999, Tom retired from Custer State Park and moved to Fort Pierre to manage a bison ranch for Ted Turner.

"I was in graduate school when I took the job as a game warden," said Tom LeFaive. "I had a biologist tech position at South Dakota State University, but I also had a wife and a child. There were not many jobs available, so I took it."

From his earliest years, Tom had an interest in wildlife.

"I never imagined I would get the chance to be a game warden," he said. "It was a dream come true, really."

The year Tom started was the year game wardens were first issued sidearms.

"They were military surplus .38 caliber revolvers," Tom recalls. "The cylinder did not line up properly with the barrel, so blow by occurred. Between the hot gas and the lead shavings, you had to wear gloves to shoot them. Later, we got .357 revolvers and then Glocks, which was a big improvement."

Tom's father taught him from a young age to love being in the outdoors. Teaching others this same lesson was his favorite part of the job.

"When I was in Aberdeen, we taught a lot of people about waterfowl hunting," said Tom. "It was an inter-agency effort – I worked with Ron Fowler, the biologist and Howard Loverien the federal wildlife agent. We all shared the same drive for education. Those who attended learned about placing decoys, identifying birds and calling. We held calling contests for the kids who came to the classes. They could win decoys and other hunting gear."

After the lessons, fathers and sons would come back to the meetings and tell Tom about successful hunts.

"'It worked!' they would tell me. 'Everything you said worked!' That was great," said Tom. "Part of being a warden at that time was teaching people to enjoy the sport in a disciplined way. My dad taught me to help people enjoy the sport. Make friends and allies through education and you will be less likely to see them in court."

Aberdeen was quite a busy community when Tom was there, which he loved.

"There was great spirit within the community," said Tom. "One year, I counted 26 out of 31 days in the month of August when I was working in the evening doing something with a club or group in the community. That didn't slow down after the big deer case we made there."

In November 1973, a conversation was overheard in a restaurant about a big deer that was shot. The gentleman in question had a tag for Perkins County.

"He couldn't go because his car broke down," said Tom. "Instead, he hunted at night with his friend along the James River."

The poached whitetail buck scored a whopping 219.25 on the Boone and Crockett scale.

He took the monster deer to the taxidermist. Little did he know the taxidermist was a former game warden and suspicious of his story.

"We waited until he paid for the mount and took it home," said Tom. "We served warrants at five locations when it went down."

When the warrants were served, officers seized the remainder of the hide that was still in the man's vehicle.

"He claimed that he killed the deer near Faith," said Tom. "But we had information otherwise."

They combed and brushed the seized hide to pull out any seeds the deer had picked up in its habitat.

"We had a botanist examined the seeds we pulled out," said Tom. "He determined that the seeds in the hide indicated the deer lived in eastern south Dakota, not west. That sealed our case."

Thinking he knew who had told on him, the guy started telling officers about violations committed by others.

"The case really snowballed when he started giving up information," said Tom.

After the deer case, Tom didn't have to go into the field looking for violations.

"People came to me," he said. "I used to take the mount to present to sportsmen's groups. I showed them this incredible deer and told them how it had been taken illegally. Seeing it really encouraged them to get involved."

In 1974, following the deer case, Tom received the Shikar Safari Officer of the Year Award. He appreciated the recognition, but Tom is adamant that conservation officers cannot do their jobs alone.

"We receive support from so many areas, both within Game, Fish & Parks as an agency and from the public," he said. "I was fortunate in my career to have great supervisors who helped me reach my potential – guys like Jack Opitz, Willie Foss, Harold Lunde and Warren Jackson. I also had incredible mentors in Howard Loverien and Dave Fisher. They were excellent, high caliber law enforcement officers. We didn't have a lot of formal training in that area when I came on, so it was important and beneficial to have support from guys like them."

Support came from all over the state, from everyone who worked in the department. A game biologist once helped prove the innocence of two men who were being investigated over some geese.

"It was springtime," recalls Tom. "I received a call from a neighboring warden. He was investigating a couple of guys caught throwing geese into the ditch, but they insisted the birds were taken legally in the fall. We needed to figure out how old the geese were to determine when they had been shot."

The pair told the investigating officer that, after hunting in the fall, they put the geese in the trunk and forgot they had them.

"As the weather warmed and they started to thaw, the rotting geese made their presence known," said Tom. "The guys were driving along, throwing the geese out and someone reported them. It still wasn't a great situation, but they insisted they had hunted the birds legally."

Tom went to Ron Fowler, game biologist, to try and find the information they needed.

"Ron had a study on tailfeather length that would tell how old the geese were," said Tom. "The guys were saying they killed the geese the week before Thanksgiving. If the story was true, the geese would have been about 18 weeks old."

Ron examined the remains and came back to Tom with what he'd found: the geese were juveniles, approximately 18 weeks old at the time of death.

"So, these guys were telling the truth," said Tom. "We got support from the biologist to prove it. We earned their respect even if they did still receive a citation for wanton waste."

That wasn't the only time Tom used science to make a case.

"We had a bighorn sheep case in Custer State Park," he recalls. "When the suspect was interviewed, they let him smoke. Of course, he left the cigarette butts. We were able to match the DNA from the cigarette butts with what was found at the scene and nailed the guy!"

It felt good to stop poachers, but Tom's true passion as a conservation officer was helping people learn how to do things so they could enjoy the outdoors.

"As a game warden, I wanted to let people know how I loved hunting and that it could be done in a disciplined manner," said Tom. "Helping people learn to do things right and helping them have a good experience is so important. I loved being that catalyst."

One year, Tom was working at the wildlife and fisheries display at the Brown County Fair. At the end of the fair, the fish were stocked in a nearby lake – it was public and popular for fishing with kids.

Taking his little girl fishing for the first time, one dad crafted a fishing pole for the youngster out of a CB antenna with an eye and a reel. They went out fishing to the stocked lake.

Soon, the little girl had something on her line. As she reeled it in, it came to the top of the water, snapping like crazy.

"Daddy, it's an alligator!" she screamed, throwing her pole and running. Dad helped her reel the fish in and called Tom to try and figure out what the thing was.

"As he described it to me, I was sure it was a gar," recalls Tom. "I told him to take it to a place called Lefty's that had a certified scale. That little girl and her CB antenna pole broke a state record!"

One of Tom's proudest moments occurred in Custer State Park, with a man and his son who was in a wheelchair.

"The boy hated school," said Tom. "His dad made a deal with him that if he did well in school they would put in for elk tags in the park."

The young man held up his end of the bargain and they submitted their applications.

They were drawn.

And Tom helped facilitate their hunt.

"I set the kid up near an active elk wallow where he could see well and was near the truck," said Tom. "His dad told him he would be just over the ridge up ahead, about 300 yards away."

There was a gunshot almost immediately.

"Dad jumped up, wondering what had happened. Was there really an elk that quickly?" said Tom. "He couldn't see his son, just the truck and an empty wheelchair. When we got to where we could see him, we realized what happened. After shooting the elk, the boy was so excited he got out of his chair and was crawling to the animal."

The emotion in Tom's voice cracks his professional veneer, if just for a moment.

"It was their dream," he said.

And it happened.

And Tom was able to help them.

"I just loved seeing people enjoying the sport of hunting."

A Close Encounter of Which Kind?

One night, a crew had come out for a spotlight patrol. Joe Marbach, the state pilot, had the plane up.

In the moonlight, Joe could see the reflection of a vehicle hood in a game production area (GPA) they were working. With all the activity around, the car still wasn't moving.

"I'll make a dive on him," said Joe over the two-way radio. "When I get close, I will turn the multi-million-candle-power search and landing lights on them. He will come out."

"The following week, I was listening to the radio," said Tom. "There was a call-in program about UFOs. A guy called in to tell his story about a close encounter with a third kind. He was in his car with his girlfriend... parked in a GPA... When something came out of nowhere."

"The UFO came down right at us and turned its ultra-bright lights on us!" the guy told the radio host emphatically.

"I did not call in to reveal the truth," said Tom with a laugh. "He's got a great story to tell and we're going to let him have it."

Carp & Cookies

"One of the West River wardens was involved in a fisheries research project," said Tom. "He had caught a carp, which he smoke and brought to share with the college research team that was coming to help with the project. Well, you know how smoked carp look…"

He had arrived at the project site early and decided to hide the fish in the grass and brush, pretending it was a several-day-old dead carp that had shriveled up in the hot sun and was quite ripe.

"With the team following him on the waterside trail, the warden acted surprised and said 'hey, a fish!'" recalls Tom. "Picking it up, he tore off a chunk and bit into it! Well, the college crew must have eaten cookies for breakfast, because they were losing a few!"

Tom laughs at the memory.

"We had fun," he said. "We worked long hours and it was hard work, but we had fun."

I Didn't Mean to be a Game Warden
Or I Left my Heart in Law Enforcement

Bob Brown began his career with South Dakota Game, Fish & Parks (SDGFP) in 1972. He was stationed in Britton during his early years and later worked in Webster, Faith and Chamberlain. He served as the assistant regional supervisor for law enforcement until 1990 and then moved over to the game side for three years. In 1993 he was promoted to regional supervisor and remained in that position until 2003. He reconsidered retirement and came back on as the boating law specialist before fully retiring in 2008.

"When I was assigned to Britton, I didn't want to be a game warden," recalls Bob. "My goal was to be a big game biologist. I had a bachelor's degree from South Dakota State University in Wildlife and Fisheries Sciences.

But, the department wasn't hiring when I graduated. By the time I realized I'd educated myself into a corner, SDSU grad school was full. Then one day, we were on our way to Sioux City for a wedding and stopped in Vermillion on the way through."

Bob was accepted to graduate school at the University of South Dakota and got a master's degree in biology.

After his thesis was finished, Bob continued working through his faculty advisor on a project for Homestake Mining – collecting information regarding mercury contamination in the Cheyenne River drainage. In the midst of collecting samples, Bob heard from SDGPF.

"I got a call late one Friday afternoon from the Wildlife Division Director asking if I wanted to go Sisseton as a game warden. Well of course I did!"

Bob was told to be in Pierre by 10 a.m. Monday morning. But by the time Monday rolled around there was a change of plans and Bob went to Britton.

"Britton was a two-man station when I started in 1972," said Bob. "Harvey Binger had been there for 15 years. He was a good fella to work with – I learned a ton from him."

In 1975, budget cuts forced the two-man station into a one-man station. Bob was transferred to Webster as a regional management specialist.

"I was supposed to be sort of a jack-of-all-trades in that role, but it really didn't turn out the way they thought it would," Bob recalls. "I kept my law enforcement certification and in 1976 I transferred to Faith as the conservation officer out there."

In December 1977, during a meeting in Rapid City, Bob was paged, along with John Wrede and Gary Goode – the Faith station, the Buffalo station and the Murdo station. They were told there were going to be budget cuts and they would be out of a job on July 1.

"Of course, nobody ever wants to hear this news," said Bob. "Somehow or another, by the spring of 1978, the new plan was to reorganize. We went from five regions to four at that time."

For management purposes, SDGFP divides the state into regions. Region 1 includes the western third of the state, Region 2 is comprised of the counties that border the Missouri River from the North Dakota border to Charles Mix County in the south. The remaining eastern third of the state is divided to make up Region 3 on the south side and Region 4 on the north side.

Prior to the reorganization, Region 2 was divided by north and south, creating five regions in the state.

"After the reorganization, there were a number of positions available, so I applied to be the assistant regional supervisor for law enforcement," said Bob. "It took me a while, but it eventually became clear that law enforcement was where my head was. I finally knew that was where I should be, not working as a big game biologist."

With this realization that he wanted to stay in law enforcement, Bob took a transfer and moved his family to Chamberlain in 1978.

"Chamberlain was a good place for us," he said. "We were able to stay here for the rest of my career; the kids were able to go to the same school all 12 years and my wife Mary taught here. It was good."

They had *how many* gallons of Smelt?!

Lake Pocasse is a federal waterfowl protection area in northern South Dakota, near Pollock and Mobridge. The lake has a water structure that flows into northern Lake Oahe.

"One year," Bob recalls, "there was a pretty decent smelt run going on. Sometimes, spawning walleye will also try to go upstream. At this particular time, there were lots of smelt to be caught. But when people would use dip nets to catch the smelt, they were also catching walleyes."

Bob and a couple other officers went up to spend some time working the area in plain clothes with an unmarked vehicle.

"One day, we came across an Asian family dip-netting smelt and doing very well," said Bob.

So well, in fact, that between the five of them they had *50 gallons* of smelt.

"At that time the limit was five gallons of smelt per person per day... so they had double their legal limit... and no licenses."

At the time, officers carried bond schedules to collect fines in the field. The schedules included court costs as well, so they were able to tell people right away what their fine would be – driving off the trail resulted in $X, no license meant $Y and so on.

The schedules also outlined the fines for being over the limit on walleye, bass and other game fish. Smelt had been inadvertently left off that year, so they fell under "All other Fish" ... which was $2 per fish.

The family had roughly 20,000 smelt.

"Well, not very many people carry $40,000 around in their wallets," said Bob. "I was trying to figure out how I could send them on their way and what I was going to do with all these fish."

Remembering they were from Bismarck, North Dakota (a fair distance away), Bob was also concerned about their gas situation.

"I certainly wasn't going to collect all their money in fines, leaving them with no gas money to get home."

Muddling through their broken English, Bob got the two men to show him their wallets. They had $50 between them.

"I collected $27 and gave them back part of the smelt," recalls Bob. "What the hell was I going to do with all those smelt?! I sent them on their way and we got back to Mobridge about 2 a.m.

The very next morning, I was back in the office with 20 gallons of smelt in the freezer when I received a call from the local Chamber of Commerce...They wanted to host a smelt feed. Could we help?"

Bob laughs at the memory and the impeccable timing of the Chamber.

"'How does 20 gallons sound?' I asked them. Come get them now, while they're fresh!

They were very grateful, but they didn't know quite how grateful I was to receive their call. It was somewhat of a miracle."

Looking Out for our Local Wardens

"Sometime in the mid-80's, we got a tip that a well-known local was 'probably' running a gill net south of Chamberlain," remembers Bob. "They were docking their boat on the Lyman County side of the river, so I got a hold of Emmett Keiser to help me out."

Conservation officers did a fair amount of night work and this was no exception. Bob and Emmett staked out where they could see the trailer and vehicle, and the lights of the boat on the river.

"Somewhere around 3 a.m. though, we fell asleep," said Bob. "When we woke up, the boat was on the trailer going down the road past us. Of course, they had no idea we were there. So we jumped in the truck and got them stopped. They didn't have any netted fish (you can tell if they have been gill-netted or not), but they were awfully curious about why we were there."

"What the hell are you guys doing up this time of night?!" they wanted to know.

"We said we were just working as usual," said Bob. "They weren't real happy, but they didn't press us anymore."

The next week, there was a letter to the editor in the local newspaper.

The next time you report us for gill netting, make sure you have the correct information. Our local game wardens need their sleep.

Always be Nice

"You never know who you might run into in the field," said Bob. "Or who they might be later in life! I found a ticket that I wrote to a guy who eventually became a commissioner. I didn't know it – he was always very cordial with me. I didn't realize it until just yesterday when I was looking for some things to share in this interview!"

Through all the ups and downs, Bob loved being a conservation officer.

"I worked with some really good guys," he said. "It was a wonderful job. It was a great time – my whole career was a great time. Of course, there were days when you would think 'well, I don't really want to do this today...' But if they called me today and asked me to come back for six months, hell, I'd be gone. I'd go. I loved it!"

I Always Wanted to be a Game Warden

By Bob Schuurmans

Bob Schuurmans began his career with South Dakota Game, Fish &
Parks as a foreman for the land crew in Mobridge. He began his train-
ing to become a conservation officer in Watertown in 1975. From there,
he was stationed in Redfield and Yankton before moving to Pierre in
1990 to manage the TIPs, law enforcement training and civil damages
programs. He retired in 2005 after 30 years with the department.

I was born and raised in South Dakota. I grew up in Wagner, in an outdoor family that spent time camping, fishing and hunting together.

I always loved the outdoors and started volunteering with the local
game warden in high school – Les Nelson out of Lake Andes. He
was great. But I also loved time spent with sportsmen. I learned con-
stantly from others about how they fished or hunted. I learned new
techniques that I would use in my job and also in my personal life.

I graduated from South Dakota State University in 1973 with degree
in Wildlife and Fisheries Sciences. While I was in college, I worked as
a park ranger in the Badlands for one summer and patrolled the back
country by horse. It was amazing! It was my first law enforcement
experience and really solidified what I wanted to do with my life.

When I started in Mobridge with the crew, I also served as a special
deputy sheriff for Walworth County.

I was involved in community organizations all through my career.
I enjoyed working as an assistant scout master while my son was

a scout. I was able to get the scouts involved in all kinds of wildlife conservation projects – building and installing wood duck houses, banding turkeys and installing fish habitat, to name a few.

I also loved meeting people from all walks of life and being able to help them in times of need. As any conservation officer will tell you, getting calls at 2 AM came with the job.

A call for an overdue boat on the Missouri River in December was a particular challenge. I had to maneuver around ice chunks for 4 miles of river with the temperature around 10 degrees before I found them... but we found them!

Another call came at midnight during a South Dakota blizzard to rescue three boys who decided to leave a party and got stuck. This was before cell phones, but they were able to find a pay phone in the state park and dial 911.

I managed to get to them but then I became stuck. We waited until a state snow plow came out to get us, leaving my pickup in a pile of snow. I spent the night in the basement of the jail because I couldn't get home.

The next day, the blizzard was still going strong and the forecast was for another day yet! An ambulance call came in for a house about two miles from mine, so I decided to hitch a ride. I hiked through the blizzard the last two miles home, but I got there!

During my years as a game warden, I worked with a local vet whose specialty was operating on small pet birds. I was able to take her injured or sick eagles I found in the area.

I loved being able to help her operate on eagles that needed to have a wing amputated. After the surgery, I would take them to the Sioux

Falls airport where the airlines would take them to a Minneapolis rehab unit. If they were able to return to the wild, we would sometimes get them back to release in our area.

If you ever get to release an eagle, MAKE SURE to look into the crate to see if everything is okay before opening it up. Also, take the stiff mailing envelope off the tail – yes, I said envelope. This was to keep the tail feathers straight during the trip.

The first time we released an eagle, we had coverage from the local news media. It could have been a unique experience to have the evening news showing an eagle taking off into the sunset... with a giant envelope stuck to its tail.

Poach Eggs, Not Wildlife

Catching poachers was a challenge I liked. No two were alike, which made the job interesting.

In the old days of pheasant hunting, you could have your gun out the window and road hunt. One day, I was working late shooters in the western part of my county, heading east as the sun went down. With the setting sun shining in your mirrors, it's hard to see me behind you, ya know.

I watched an older car slowly going down a county road that was known for this type of hunting. As I followed the car, it went over a hill so I sped up to get closer.

As I approached the top of the hill, I saw the car was stopped. A guy was just going over the fence out in the field. He came back to the fence with a rooster.

I met him and asked for his license. He immediately said "you got me."

Well, I hadn't seen what happened. I was totally caught by surprise and had no idea what to say.

"Tell me about it," I said to him.

"Well, you saw me shoot it with a .22 rifle out the car window and you know I don't have a license."

That had to be fastest confession I had ever had.

Some Cases Land in your Lap, Others Land on your Vehicle

It was deer season and unseasonably warm. I was nearing a stop sign and there was a pickup in front of me. I was guessing they had been out hunting, but didn't know for sure. As we approached the stop sign together, an arm came out the driver's side window.

CLUNK!

An empty beer can unceremoniously landed on the hood of my truck. I didn't need to turn on my lights to let them know they were being stopped. As I approached the vehicle, the driver was apologetic.

"That's the worst sounding clunk I've ever heard in my life!" he said sheepishly.

One sunny Monday morning, after working duck hunter blinds on the Missouri River, I was heading to town and decided to take a short road down to the river. I observed three guys hunting out of a duck blind when a flock of redheads flew by me, made a swoop out over the river and flew right past the blind.

All three hunters shot at them and one duck fell.

I had just checked the group two days before and had given each of them duck ID books – I figured they were good. I was about to leave when I noticed the guy who went out into the decoys to retrieve the fallen duck was now holding it up and twisting it all around to observe it from every angle… like he was trying to identify it.

I stayed put and watched as he went back into the blind. All of them were now looking at it. The guy holding the duck left the blind again.

Mind you, they were on a bare sandbar where an ant could not hide. But, I watched him hunch over (as if that made him smaller) and bury the duck.

I thought for sure they would see me – I was only 400 yards away in sunlight. But, I went back to my shed, retrieved my boat and went out to the sandbar.

When I arrived, they had five other ducks in the blind.

"I am sure you have six ducks," I told them, pulling out my notebook, pretending I had watched them and had notes (which I didn't).

They all stated they only had five ducks. The hunter who buried the duck was standing in front of me so I took a step closer… he backed up. Again, I took a step and he moved away from me.

I did this until he was standing on top of the buried duck.

At that point I said "I know where that other duck is – you are standing on it."

His eyes got as big as paper plates and looked like a deer in headlights.

He dug up the duck. I had him wash it off and asked him to tell me what it was. All three hunters stated they did not know. The duck ID books I had given to them two days before were at home. Being afraid of taking an illegal duck, they buried it.

Had they kept it – and known their ducks – they would have been fine.

Even the best laid plans don't always go as planned. I was with a US Fish & Wildlife agent working a group of hunters in the river bottoms near Springfield, South Dakota. We had taken up use of a duck blind not far away from the group we suspected to be over-bagging.

We had set up a spotting scope on the door of the blind and had our binoculars laying on the front when a boat showed up. It was a guy from Nebraska.

"What are you doing in my blind?" he asked.

In those days you could leave a permanent blind on the Missouri River year-round. If the hunter was not using it that day, you could. If the owner showed up, you just had to find a different blind.

Of course, we wanted to accommodate this gentleman and follow the rules. As we loaded our equipment to move, and he was putting his into the blind, I asked him for his license.

He looked very surprised. "Have I been hunting yet?" he asked.

"No, I suppose you have not," I answered. He took that moment to let me know he would be leaving to go buy his federal duck stamp.

Working road checks can have its rewards. A few of my fellow officers and I were working a specific area with the hope that a certain fisherman would be coming through.

He did not show up that day but, as we were shutting down and the other officers had just left, I saw one more boat coming through that stopped. It was a couple from Omaha, Nebraska.

By the time I got all their fish counted, they were 87 walleyes over the limit.

In those days, if a non-resident could not post the bond as set by the court, you had to take them in. Which I did.

On the way to town, I had the gentleman in my vehicle while his wife drove his. I asked why he did it. He was mad at this wife – they had been fishing for three days and she would not let him cook any of the fish. She made him go out and get more than his limit each day until she figured they had enough for a neighborhood fish fry.

When we got to town, I felt sorry for him – bond was going to be over $600 and they didn't have it on them. This meant he would sit in jail until they did. Because all the credit cards were in his name, she could not go to the bank and get any money. (Wow, have things changed today! I think the first thing my wife did when we got married was get credit cards in her name!)

Anyway, I took him over to the bank to get cash for bond. The teller asked him what he needed the money for and he pointed at me in uniform. I advised her it was for his bond, or he had to stay in jail.

I can't say I think it was a pleasant 3-hour ride home for them.

Poached Elk Lead to TIPs Program

By Bob Hauk

Bob Hauk began his career with South Dakota Game, Fish & Parks in 1972 as a conservation officer (CO) in Faith, South Dakota. He transferred to the Rapid City CO position in 1975. He worked in this position from 1972-1983 when he became the TIPs Coordinator. After three years in that role he became the game management supervisor for Region 1 in Rapid City. In the fall of 2000, he retired after 29 years of service to SDGFP. Bob shares the story about how TIPs, or Turn In Poachers, began.

In the fall of 1983, I was the conservation officer for Rapid City. In early November of that year, we received a call about two dead elk south of Deerfield Lake. Another officer went to take a look and observed that there were indeed two dead bull elk with what appeared to be bullet holes in them. An examination the following morning provided two bullets – one from each animal.

Somehow, word got around about these two nice bull elk that had been shot and left. Over coffee a few mornings later, several individuals got together and decided to raise some money to post as a reward for the arrest and conviction of those responsible.

The story made front page of the *Rapid City Journal.*

Within a few days this small group had raised $3,000 dollars to offer a reward in the case, again making front page news. Within a week, I received two calls from different individuals with information regarding the elk.

The first caller knew all the information I needed. He even knew the rifle used and where I would find the weapon in a particular gun case downstairs in the residence.

The second caller had no firsthand information but had heard the story, including the names of those involved. This was possibly bar talk, I do not know, but bragging will get you every time. But the interesting thing was, the names were the same. So we had corroboration from two different individuals, unknown to one another, providing the same names of those responsible.

Now, the two bull elk in question were killed near Deerfield Lake but the location has, at least anecdotally, come to be known as Palmer's Gulch. The last name of the defendant in this case was, you guessed it, Palmer. Perhaps this explains how it got to be that they were killed in Palmer's Gulch.

At any rate, the information provided through these phone calls was sufficient for me to obtain search warrants for the residences of both individuals named.

The warrants were served at both residences at the same time one evening by myself and several other officers. We left with two weapons of the same caliber, one from each place. I took the rifles and the bullets from the elk to the crime lab in Pierre. Several months passed, but finally we heard back that both bullets were fired from the same gun and both matched one of the rifles – Palmer's!

The story went that the driver of the vehicle killed the first bull. When the second bull only ran a short distance, both individuals got out of the pickup and shot at it.

What we lost with this ballistics report is any evidence to clearly link the second individual to the crime. He was lucky. One of three things had to have happened:

1) He missed the elk

2) His bullet passed through the elk and we did not retrieve it

3) He simply did not shoot at the elk

What we gained from this report was clear evidence of one individual's rifle killing both elk. He had also previously admitted to carrying that rifle while deer hunting in the Black Hills that particular day.

Now we have front page news again.

A lot of people were upset with the useless killing and wasting of these elk. Many sportsmen thought "there goes another one of my chances to ever draw a Black Hills elk tag."

Next, the defendant got a lawyer and plead not guilty. The not guilty plea led to more front page news.

We had a preliminary hearing with the crime lab expert from Pierre testifying along with the rest of us. Every time more information came out or we went to court: more news.

Poor Palmer would have his name on both the front page of the *Rapid City Journal* and the evening news over and over again.

Sufficient evidence was found to take the case to jury trail. In the end, he plead guilty just before going to trail. More news.

And you know what? I do not even remember what his sentence was now. I do remember he was making payments to the court for some time.

The successful outcome of this case rallied area sportsmen. They went to Pierre and asked administration to consider starting a program that would use donated dollars to pay for information to help reduce the illegal taking of wildlife.

In the course of these efforts, I was asked if this money helped to solve this particular case. I said it was the only thing that did it.

I was in the right place at the right time and, shortly thereafter, became the first Turn In Poachers or TIPs coordinator for South Dakota.

Only a few other states had such a program in place in the early 1980's. New Mexico had what they called Operation Game Thief. I spent a considerable amount of time meeting with them and organizing our program in a similar manner. Today, I believe just about every state has a program like TIPs.

In the beginning, we raised more money than we were paying out in rewards, so the program grew quickly. After initially being only a pilot program in the Black Hills area, it went statewide three years later in 1986. I left the program at that time and became the assistant regional game management supervisor in Rapid City.

I'm pleased to say the TIPS program is going strong to this day!

Meet Bob Gray & Dave Brown

Conservation officers in South Dakota often helped each other out as neighbors and comrades in law enforcement. Sometimes their efforts required an unknown face in a particular area. Bob Brown and Dave Gray worked together to help Owen Meadows crack a case near Edgemont in the early 1990s.

"Well these boys… not boys, men, were out of Edgemont," remembers Owen. "I had pretty good knowledge of the fact that they were taking too many big game animals and maybe doing it without a license."

Owen began the investigation, but it was going nowhere.

"I decided to see about getting a couple game wardens there in plain clothes to see if we could figure anything out that way," said Owen. "Dave Gray and Bob Brown came to Fall River County and they wandered into the bar."

"The guys Owen told us about weren't hard to find," said Bob. "One was an alcoholic pool hustler with a pretty unique manner of speech. The other was the grandson of a Tennessee game warden. He would talk all the time about hoping his grandpa never found out what he was doing up here in South Dakota."

Lee Vanderbush was also there the first night but, in the days and nights that followed, it was just Dave and Bob.

"When we found them in the pool hall that first night, they wanted to play for money," said Bob. "We said we weren't good enough for that, but would play for a beer or something. So we introduce ourselves – Dave was Dave Brown and I was Bob Gray… it's almost embarrassing to tell the story now.

In that environment, you need a name that at least comes out right. I don't think that Owen was real impressed with our efforts here. I guess I'm not anymore either.

We were able to make arrangements to meet the next morning to go hunting though, so that's what mattered."

The suspects had left the pool hall and Bob and Dave were playing a couple more games of pool when another guy came walking up to them.

"You guys look like a couple game wardens," he said.

"Mm, no. We're not," Bob and Dave replied, keeping their cool.

"Well, what the hell do you do?" the stranger asked Bob.

"I'm an unemployed guitar player," he said.

"Well there's a guitar over there, go get it."

"If you want me to play guitar, you go get it," was Bob's reply.

"Then he looks at Dave and wants to know what he does," said Bob. "I said I was a guitar player because I can at least play the guitar. But Dave, he says 'I'm a surveyor for the Department of Transportation.' I'm standing there wondering if Dave knows squat about DOT…"

"Laser or other?" the stranger wanted to know.

"Laser," says Dave, cool as a cucumber.

"I still have no idea if Dave knew anything about lasers or not," recalls Bob. "But it satisfied this guy."

Pretty soon, Dave Brown and Bob Gray had made a new friend and were driving around the country with him.

"He came up with some other information that really turned out to be worthless," said Bob. "But it was an interesting day!"

Dave and Bob met up with their suspects the next morning as planned. After a couple hunting excursions, there still wasn't much happening.

"When we got back that night I talked them into giving us a half a turkey they had poached," said Bob. "We gave it to Owen and he went the next day and dropped the hammer. So that was the deal, it came together."

When they were done working these guys, Bob, Dave and Owen got together to write their statements.

Owen was a bit puzzled by the names they had chosen for the operation.

"You guys were just plain-clothes, not so much under cover," said Owen. "But you couldn't come up with anything better than Brown and Gray?!"

A Whole New Set of Stories

By Chris Kuntz

Chris began his career with South Dakota Game, Fish & Parks in 2010, just two months after graduating from Colorado State University with a degree in Natural Resource Management and a minor in Fish Biology. He was stationed in Huron for seven years before transferring to Sioux Falls.

Every conservation officer, no matter what state or country they work in, has great stories to be told. With all of these stories, have you ever wondered how they got started?

Over my years as a conservation officer, there is one question that continually comes up, whether it's at a school presentation or from someone who comes out for a day to shadow me on the job.

"What made you want to become a conservation officer?"

Hunting, fishing and enjoying the great outdoors are things that every conservation officer probably loves to do. After that, there could be countless reasons why people become conservation officers. For me, it ultimately came down to a 12-year-old girl losing her hand in a boat accident.

This answer typically shocks people. They expect an answer about wanting to work outside and save wildlife... but this is my story.

As a kid growing up, I spent a lot of time on my family's farms in North Dakota and would go fishing every chance I got. In middle school, after my family moved to northern Colorado, my dad was traveling a lot. At that time, I took an interest in airplanes and was certain I wanted to be a pilot.

Well, that all changed thanks to a high school instructor named Craig, whom I got to know through a group called Colorado Youth Outdoors. Colorado Youth Outdoors gives high school students and their parents opportunities to learn about various outdoor topics – fishing, rod building (something I still do to this day), archery, shotgun sports and many more – in an effort to help get parents and students involved in something together and build a bond between them.

One day late in my freshman year, Craig approached me and said, "Hey, if you're interested I have a summer job you might like."

It turned out the job was a boat assistant, which essentially was a person who helped out the seasonal boat rangers at the local state park. Now this really sparked my interest. I had spent a fair amount of time fishing on boats growing up and always enjoyed it, but I knew nothing about law enforcement regarding boats.

Craig had been working at the park for a number of years and offered me the opportunity to do a ride along with one of the boat rangers that summer to see what it was like.

I took him up on the offer and what an afternoon it would be.

After showing me around the lake and contacting some boats to check for violations, we were on a stop that would change my life.

The three of us on the patrol boat were occupied with a boat we had stopped when we heard someone yell from behind us.

"Her hand is gone!"

Turning around, we were greeted by a jet ski pulling up and a frantic dad handing over his 12-year-old daughter. She was missing her hand.

After some quick instructions telling Dad to head to the marina, we headed for shore. Craig put me to work getting out medical supplies to begin first aid.

Now, you are probably wondering what could possibly make this a positive story.

We came to find out that Dad was able to locate the girl's hand tangled in a rope. Thanks to a delay in the ambulance's arrival, he was able to send the hand along to the hospital. I would later learn that they were able to re-attach the hand and she got some function back.

Keep in mind that, when this happened, I was only 14-years-old. You can imagine the look on my parents faces when they came to pick me up!

Watching all the park rangers and emergency medical staff work together to help this girl was fascinating. I knew then that I wanted to work in this field.

The following three summers, I was employed by Colorado State Parks. This came with many new experiences, including meeting the local wildlife conservation officers and learning about their jobs.

That first summer would ultimately make me want to work in natural resource law enforcement. During my senior year in high school, I was able to do a number of ride alongs with wildlife conservation officers around northern Colorado, which helped solidify my decision to pursue what I believe is the best job in law enforcement.

After my freshman year in college, I took a job as a seasonal boat ranger with the Larimer County Department of Natural Resources. I would stay there for three summers, experiencing law enforcement on the water and responding to boat and vehicle accidents, as well as various medical calls including rattle snake bites and falls from cliffs. I also helped patrol a number of camp grounds and day use areas.

In February 2010, I began my training at the law enforcement academy in Pierre – I was about to be a conservation officer... And that's where a whole new set of stories begins.

When the Camo Works Too Well

Forrest Lewis began his career with South Dakota Game, Fish & Parks in 1979 as a state trapper. In 1982, he became a wildlife conservation officer, working in Harding County and Lyman County. Health issues spurred his retirement in 1992.

"This little story..." Forrest begins with a chuckle. "We had to patrol on the big [Missouri] River and the White River as part of our territory in that area. One evening, I had a fellow call up and say 'Forest, I'm just getting robbed. They're taking all my fish and cutting some of my traps loose or taking them somewhere else.'

So he's losing traps and fish. He wanted to know if I'd come down there and see if we could do something about it.

Well, we talked a little bit more and he told me some things about how many fish he thought he was losing and I called another conservation officer (CO) out of Chamberlain. We called him Down the Creek Jack because there was a Jack up north and one south, so the guy I worked with in my area was Down the Creek Jack.

Anyway, Jack and I got up early morning, went over there before the sun came up and it got light. We figured out where everything was – the camp setup along the river and all that. We walked in about a half a mile and got on the side of a hill in some brush and watched this camp.

I told the fisherman who'd called to report the crimes to stay out of the area for about two days. Leave it alone and we'll see what we can gather up, so we thought we were looking at the thieves in their camp.

Starting at light, one guy got up for the morning. He got out of the tent, walked over toward the river. He stretched a little bit and relieved himself right there alongside the river.

We watched him walk around and he went to some freezers. So we thought maybe there was fish in them and started figuring out just how we were going to do this, going in to the camp to talk to them.

Pretty soon another guy came out and was standing there. Jack said 'Forrest, I'm going to run down there and try to get into a place where I can maybe hear some of the conversation.'

So he starts sneaking over there with his camouflage and stuff, and he got over there just alongside a patch of brush. All the sudden, the second guy turned and stretched and started walking right towards Jack. I thought for sure he'd seen him.

Jack's looking at me, and he's snuggling down more into that bush as the guy approached. He shook his hands like 'Quiet! Don't move! Don't do nothin'!'

That guy walked up there and had to be within about three feet of Jack. I don't know why he couldn't see a guy laying in that bush, except Jack had all that fancy camo stuff on him. That guy turned around and looked back toward the river, and he started unbuckling his britches."

Forrest laughs out loud at the memory.

"That ol' boy stood there and he got his britches down and squats. He had to be within three feet of Jack's head. I had to put a stick in my mouth because I was laughing so cotton pickin' hard!

Jack had looked at me and put his hands over his eyes and every now and then he'd flip me that 'IQ' sign. I just, I tell you what, I bit that stick in half watching him squirm as that ol' boy wiped his butt and stood up and finally walked off.

I can't begin to express the way Jack wiggled his nose, wiggled his mouth, tried to plug his ears and keep from laughing... it was a hee haw!

So Jack starts sneaking back up the hill – he wasn't going to stay next to that pile anymore. We went off a ways and got him all cooled out from the ordeal and then we went back to get our job done.

We made quite a case of it. They had fish they took off the set lines and the trot lines, and out of those little catfish boxes. They got hit pretty hard.

Just a couple years ago I saw Jack. Right away he says 'don't be telling me about that thing on the White River!'"

Forrest laughs again, enjoying the memory.

"So Jack was a good hand about it and it was quite a story."

The Tennessee Trio

Dan Plut began his career with South Dakota Game, Fish & Parks in June 1972 in Freeman, South Dakota. In June 1977, he moved to Aberdeen where he stayed until 1983. That year, he accepted a position as assistant regional supervisor position, law enforcement, and moved to Sioux Falls where he retired in July 1998. After a year on the sidelines, Dan went back on a contract basis in 1999 to man the Plankinton area in the summer and fall, as well as doing some other work around the region. He is now fully retired and he and his wife Connie live in Brandon.

In 1987, for the first time in anyone's memory, South Dakota took measures to extradite hunters for wildlife violations. Three hunters from Tennessee had poached deer and waterfowl, and even stopped in Missouri on their way to South Dakota to hunt turkeys out of season. A photograph taken by a Missouri farm woman would later help add these counts to the federal wildlife violations against them, including transporting illegally taken game across state lines.

It all began in the late spring of 1985, when Conservation Officer Dan Plut was contacted about a guy named Lowell.

"My informant told me this guy served as a hunting guide in Beadle County," said Dan. "But he was kind of an all-around game thief and renegade. Lowell had a reputation. He was a bad person. Everyone was scared to death of him."

The informant wanted to talk and trusted Dan, but was afraid of what might happen if his name was brought into it.

"He didn't want me to go ahead with the case if his name could get brought up in any way, shape or form," Dan recalls. "I told him it would be okay. But we knew each other. So I told him, the only thing is, if you see me around town, don't even acknowledge that I exist. And if you ever see me with Lowell, just turn around and get the hell outta there."

Dan got all the information he could from the informant, which was enough to start the investigation.

"I talked to Wally Davis in Pierre and let him know I thought we really needed to go ahead on this and Wally fully agreed," Dan said. "At that time, we had no investigators. However, I had gone through the undercover investigations training at the Federal Law Enforcement Training Center down in Glynco, Georgia.

So, I went up to Beadle county, kind of freelancing it, and I started looking for places for 'my boss and his wife' to come up and hunt. I went to a number of farms around the one that belonged to Lowell's father. Finally, I stopped there.

'My bosses aren't here,' I told him. 'I'm up doing some work for them. But they are going to be here for pheasant season, up from Kansas City. They've got some dollars to play with and they are looking for a decent place to hunt.'

'You probably need to talk to my son,' the man told me. 'He does some guiding. He has some other guys come up too. Maybe he would be willing to add you to their group if he can.'

'That would be ideal,' I said with a smile."

Through this conversation, Dan learned about Lowell's other group.

"He used to host quite a few hunters and had a group from down south."

Tennessee, to be exact.

The group of three consisted of an attorney and magistrate who had been an FBI agent, his son who was part owner of a tire store, and a friend – Dexter Senior, Dexter Junior and Andy.

"I had a name and phone number set up to use for the investigation," Dan recalls. "So, I get a call on that line and it's Lowell. We decided to meet one evening to discuss my proposition.

I had an old pickup to drive and, on the night we were supposed to meet, I went to his house west of Huron. He jumped in with me and we went to the bowling alley for supper.

We were kind of in a corner, but I was looking around and saw that I knew some people in there. And as we're talking I realize I knew some other people. Damn, I knew THOSE people too!

It was packed that night and I finally said 'Lowell, is there a place a little quieter we can talk about stuff?'

'Well, there's the Airport, but that's kind of spendy.'

'Let's go,' I said."

Dan spent the next couple hours buying Lowell drinks and a great big steak, and listening to everything Lowell wanted to talk about.

"I just kept listening," said Dan. "There's something called predisposition to do something. If we can establish that a guy is predisposed to commit a crime – in other words, if he would do it on his own or has admitted to doing it in the past – it's not entrapment to let him do it again, or to give him the opportunity to do it again. He admitted all kinds of stuff to me. Old Lowell, he liked to brag."

Dan learned a lot about Lowell that night, but he also learned about the group from Tennessee who would soon make their annual appearance in South Dakota.

"They would come up and hunt with Lowell and bring a big freezer with them," said Dan. "The story was that they would buy a beef when they were here, so that was the reason for the freezer. They would poach deer during pheasant season, turns out, along with waterfowl and turkeys every year. Everything would be wrapped like it came from a locker and stamped *BEEF*. They would buy some actual beef from a locker and scatter it on top of the illegal game in the bottom. And away they would go, all the way back to Tennessee."

Dan and Lowell made arrangements for Dan to return on the opening weekend of pheasant season, with his "bosses" in tow. Everyone would hunt pheasants with Lowell as their guide.

Arlo Haase, the conservation officer from Grant County and a federal agent named Cindy Schroeder would pose as Dan's husband-and-wife bosses.

Finally, opening weekend arrived.

"We found out the guys from Tennessee couldn't come opening weekend, they were coming later," said Dan. "But we'd been talking about them. The old man, Dexter Senior, had a couple of fancy dogs – French Brittany spaniels."

With this news, plan B kicked in.

"'Is there any chance we could come up and hunt with those dogs?' I asked Lowell. 'I just love them and I've never hunted over dogs before.'"

"I think I could arrange that," said Lowell jiggling his head in approval.

"The truth was, if you paid him enough money, he would arrange anything," said Dan.

With that settled, Dan, Arlo and Cindy still had the opportunity to hunt with Lowell and his cohorts opening weekend of pheasant season, on land that belonged to Lowell's dad.

"We all got together Saturday morning. We had three cars in our group and we were following them along.

We started out hunting a federal area and shot a few pheasants. Then we went to some land along the James River. When we got there, Lowell's buddy Rick came running up.

'Here!'

He handed me two OO Buckshot. He gave Arlo two as well.

'These are for deer!' he said. 'If you see deer, use this, it will knock them down.'"

As they hunted along the river, a pheasant got up and swung wide. Dan let it get over the river and then killed it. The wind was blowing and pushed it to the other side.

Lowell stalked up, angry at Dan.

"What'd you shoot it over there for?" he demanded.

"He was in range," Dan said. "We have not seen that many pheasants, so I shot it. My fault."

"Well I'll go get the goddamn thing," muttered Lowell.

"So, Lowell took off to drive around section lines and cross a bridge and get the pheasant. He wasn't there when the first deer was shot," remembers Dan.

"We kept hunting a few corn patches. As we were walking, Arlo was to my right. All the sudden, Rick hollers 'deer, deer!'

Two shots later, someone hollers 'we got him!'"

They had shot a deer, alright, on the opening day of *pheasant* season. With two undercover conservation officers and a federal agent in their hunting party… It wouldn't be the last deer poached before the investigation came to an end.

"We start walking up to that deer," remembers Dan. "We were probably about 20 feet from them. Arlo was closest and we're kind of cutting across the field, arcing over to where Lowell's two buddies are with the deer they just killed.

All of the sudden, Rick jumps up and comes running up to Arlo with his gun. He ran right to Arlo's face.

'Alright game warden, what the hell ya gonna do about it?!' he yelled."

Dan froze; the hair stood up on the back of his neck.

"I was 20 feet away when Rick hollered. Somehow, I thought, we must have got into trouble and this is going bad really fast. Right then, I knew if Rick started moving the gun towards Arlo, I was going to shoot him.

I stopped right where I was. I'm carrying a gun, and I'm ready to shoot Rick.

Arlo, I still remember, he starts laughing.

With Rick in his face, he laughs and he says 'Jesus Christ, wouldn't that be something though?'

Then Rick started laughing.

'Boy, it sure as hell would!' said Rick, still laughing. Then Chuck came over and he thought it was funny too. It was all a joke. Arlo's reaction was perfect. They had no clue who we really were."

It was all a joke and everyone was laughing … but the wardens felt warm under the collar.

Dan turned around and caught Arlo's eye, phew!

"We were very relieved," said Dan.

Later that night Dan and Arlo talked about the incident.

"Dan, my heart went from about 80 beats per minute to 180 beats in one second!" said Arlo. "I was going to hit him with the butt of my gun. There wasn't room to get it up, and Rick's gun was already part way up."

Dan assured him, "Arlo, if he had moved that gun another inch toward you, I was going to shoot him."

"I would have been thankful if you had," Arlo replied.

Though rattled, everyone was okay and their cover was not blown. The investigation would continue.

When Lowell got back with the pheasant Dan had shot, the deer had been gutted out in the field. The deer went into Lowell's basement.

"We kept on hunting Saturday and Sunday and got a few more pheasants," said Dan. "All the while, Lowell kept talking. Cindy was an excellent undercover officer and it didn't take much for her to get Lowell to try to impress her with his stories."

When Dan, Arlo and Cindy left their guide, they had illegal deer meat and other evidence. They had also made arrangements to come back in November to hunt with the group from Tennessee, which had been their original intent.

When the weekend finally came, Dan, Arlo and Cindy got into town early and stayed at a different hotel than Lowell's southern friends.

"Dexter Senior was ex-FBI, an attorney and a magistrate. He was an unlikable loudmouth, but his son was worse," said Dan. "The son bragged about shooting a deer in Smoky Mountain National Park and leaving the guts in the birdbath at a park ranger's residence.

They had poached turkeys in Missouri on their way to South Dakota. They even had pictures! Cindy got them to give us a picture, which we were able to document and add to the charges."

After hunting all day Saturday, everyone went out to eat. After dinner, the plan was for everyone to go spotlighting for deer. A stop at a filling station nearly blew their cover again.

"Lowell filled up with gas and went in to pay for it and buy some booze," said Dan. "I wanted to be sure to stay on his good side, so I followed him in and handed him four or five $20 bills. When he thanked me, the guy in front of him in line glanced back at us.

It was Carl Haberstick, the assistant state's attorney from Beadle County who, of course, didn't know we were there. Nobody knew we were there.

In hindsight, he was an excellent prosecutor for our case, but I wasn't very happy to see him at that moment.

Now, the last time I had seen this guy, he was defending a case that I was involved with – kind of a serious deer case down in Hutchinson

County. He knew who I was and what I did for a living. But the thing about this guy... he was blind in one eye.

It was that eye that was turned my way. When I saw who it was, I headed straight for the back of the store, ducked around a couple aisles and headed back out to the vehicle.

That's the problem when you're working in your home country, right?"

After only two evenings and one full day with Dexter Senior, Dexter Junior and Andy, Dan never saw them in the field again. He had, however, witnessed them, their buddy Lowell and Lowell's local buddies killing deer without licenses, spotlighting deer, trespassing and shooting out the window of a moving vehicle.

All in all, they had poached five deer, wounded at least two more and taken shots at seven or eight, all out of season and most with the help of a spotlight. Of course, this was in addition to turkeys in Missouri and a couple buckets of ducks.

It was time to act.

"Sunday morning, Arlo and Cindy went to Lowell's house to collect the deer he had for us and pay him for the hunt," said Dan. "I spent all morning typing and rushed to meet the judge in order to get the search warrant issued.

I met Judge Hoyt in a parking lot near his church as he was leaving the service. He knew Lowell and his reputation, and was a hunter himself.

As he read through the affidavit and search warrant, his smile got bigger and bigger. He signed it all right there in the parking lot where I met him – we didn't even go to the courthouse.

'Boy, it's about time you guys got onto this guy,' Judge Hoyt told me."

While Dan obtained search warrants, officers were gathering to serve them.

"There were quite a few guys," Dan recalls. "We had enough officers to cover everything we needed – photographer, everything."

From previous visits, Dan knew that Lowell kept loaded guns around the house. An obvious danger to his two young boys, the weapons were also of primary concern to the officers serving the search warrants.

"They found the guns first and secured them immediately," said Dan. "Lowell sat in his chair, guarded by two officers, and watched as they went over everything. They took mounted antlers, equipment he used to snag walleye, everything that was used to commit the crimes against wildlife he had bragged about."

Meanwhile, there was no sign of Dexter Senior, Dexter Junior or their friend Andy.

But, part of Dan's morning mission had been to get all the information to Bob Schuurmans, the conservation officer in Yankton at the time.

As the warrants were served, officers from many branches of law enforcement were posted east of Sioux Falls and on Interstate 29 south of Sioux Falls, as well as a full team in Yankton and going into Nebraska. Everyone was looking for a Chevy Suburban from Tennessee hauling a freezer. Dan never saw them pass by his post near Mitchell.

It was dark and he was worried.

"Finally," said Dan, "I got the call from Bob saying they had them stopped just over the river in Nebraska. I ran like hell from Mitchell down to Yankton."

They had them. But the adventure was not over yet.

Dexter Senior was ex-FBI. He was an attorney and magistrate. He would not go quietly. He claimed entrapment, offered bribes, called in favors and used every weapon in his crooked arsenal to get out of the charges.

"The next day at the courthouse, this FBI agent comes up and tells me we need to talk," said Dan. "He has a legal pad full of notes – Dexter Senior has been up all night making up stories and documenting everything that we 'did to him.' He had quite an imagination.

The FBI agent even went so far as to read me my Miranda warning. I asked if I was under arrest. When he said no, I left. I warned Cindy what had happened and told Arlo not to say a word to him."

Dexter Senior's efforts were wasted, however.

Jeff Stingley, Secretary of South Dakota Game, Fish & Parks at the time, was highly interested in the case and he wasn't the only one. The Game Fish & Parks Commission also took a stand, according to a statement made for a newspaper interview by Carl Haberstick, who had become the state's attorney for Beadle county.

Interestingly, the night of the arrest, Dan called his boss, Wally, to inform him of the events that had unfolded. Wally was also very interested in the case and decided to call Secretary Stingley... who was having dinner with then-governor Bill Janklow.

In the end, Lowell was fined $1,950. He served over a year of jail time with work release and was on probation for five years, during which he could not hunt or fish.

Lowell's local buddies, who participated in taking the first illegal deer of the investigation, each paid $262 in fines and $450 in jailing fees. The shooter who actually killed the deer paid an additional $1,000. On top of the fines, they served 15 days of jail time with work release and lost their hunting privileges for a year.

Dexter Senior posted $3,500 bond in Beadle County for himself, Dexter Junior and Andy, which was forfeited when they did not return for court. The three were eventually charged with 22 state violations along with federal crimes including violating the Migratory Treaty Act, unlawful taking and possession of migratory birds and violations of the Lacey Act, which involves transporting illegally taken wildlife across state lines.

Each man pleaded guilty and paid fines according to the charges against them: Dexter Senior paid $3,000, Dexter Junior paid $4,000 and Andy paid $2,000. They also served jail time, but were not required to come back to South Dakota to do so.

This was a widely followed case, both in South Dakota and Tennessee, with several articles appearing in the *Knoxville Journal*. Jaciel Woster of the South Dakota Attorney General's office at the time, is quoted in a newspaper article noting how smoothly things had gone.

"Traditionally, governors' offices are not especially willing to extradite on a misdemeanor," she said. "For some reason, they agreed to the extradition on these three men without much reticence."

Indeed, it was the first state extradition to South Dakota involving wildlife violations. The case also sparked the creation of investigator positions within SDGFP. Those specialized positions still exist and the individuals filling them continue to make cases to protect South Dakota wildlife.

It took a citizen who finally became more fed up with wildlife violations than afraid of the man committing them.

It took an officer he trusted more than he was daunted by his fear.

It took three undercover agents two weekends, many nights, countless phone conversations and one really good scare to complete the investigation.

It took a boss having faith in his officer that it was the right time to pursue the tip.

It took officers upon officers to serve search warrants and cover highways in every direction to close the net.

It took a boss, who willing to go to the next boss, who was willing to go to the Game Fish & Parks Commission and to the Governor of South Dakota.

All these people, backing each other, stood up and said "South Dakota doesn't stand for this anymore."

"This is why we are game wardens," said Dan. "This is what we do."

Getting the Pickle

By Bob Hauk

Bob Hauk began his career with South Dakota Game, Fish & Parks in 1972 as a conservation officer (CO) in Faith, South Dakota. He transferred to the Rapid City CO position in 1975. He worked in this position from 1972-1983 when he became the TIPs Coordinator. After three years in that role he became the game management supervisor for Region 1 in Rapid City. In the fall of 2000, he retired after 29 years of service to SDGFP.

One Saturday I was on routine patrol at Pactola Lake checking fishing licenses. I came across a middle-aged woman sitting in a chair on the shoreline with two fishing lines in the water. Alongside her were a tackle box, bait and several trout on a stringer in the water near by — she was obviously fishing.

After exchanging pleasantries, I asked to see her fishing license. She dug around for a while and when she could not come up with one, she told me she remembered leaving it at home. All the while, she continued to emphatically insist that she did, in fact, have a license.

Not wanting to leave the lake and not wanting to drive 30 miles back to Rapid to check her license, I offered a deal.

"I will write you a ticket for fishing without a license, but if you bring your license to the Game, Fish & Parks office Monday morning and show me I will not file the ticket. She agreed and signed the ticket. She said she knew right were the office was and I would see her by 10A.M. on Monday morning.

Remember, this was back in the "old" days – a decade before I'd even heard of a computer or anything about checking information in the field. We did not even have cell phones yet.

Sure enough, Monday and Tuesday came and went with no middle-aged lady ever showing up at the office to show me a fishing license.

It was time for a little detective work. I had written down her name, her date of birth and the address she had given me.

First, I found out that no driver's license had ever been issued in South Dakota to a person by that name and date of birth. Then, I discovered the address she gave was close but not close enough. The street was there, but there was no such numbered house on that street.

I sat on this ticket for a while but, at the end of the year, I was cleaning up old cases and came across it again. I finally filled my report to Pierre.

On the disposition form I wrote "This lady wins an Oscar and I get the pickle. No such person, no such address in Rapid City. Live and learn."

January is the Best

Dennis (Dennie) Mann began his career with SDGFP in 1977 as a habitat technician in Spearfish. In 1981 he became a wildlife conservation officer (WCO) and moved to Murdo. In 1994 he moved to Rapid City, where he spent seven years as the assistant regional supervisor. He retired in 2012 after serving the last 10 years of his career as a regional habitat manager.

I was home on a Friday night in January watching TV when the Jones County Sheriff's office called and asked if I could meet at their office. I arrived and found that two guys and a gal had been arrested. They were traveling from Montana back to Florida … with three 35-gallon barrels filled with deer quarters.

The trio had stopped at the rest area in Jackson County. There were no paper towels, so they decided to tear the dispenser off the bathroom wall. A truck driver witnessed the vandalism and called 911. Keep in mind, this was before cell phones. The truck driver made the call from a pay phone, which every rest area had.

If not for this concerned citizen, they probably would have made it back to Florida.

The vandals were pulled over at the Murdo exit. When deputies discovered the deer and firearms, they arrested them and called me to assist.

They had a "MAC 10" 9mm in the door panel, two HK 91 rifles and Steiner binoculars in the vehicle, along with all the deer.

The Lacey Act of 1900 prohibits the trafficking of illegal wildlife. Because they had transported the poached deer across state lines, this was a clear violation. It was now a federal issue, so I called John Cooper, our federal agent in Pierre, to assist with the arrest. John made the quick trip from Pierre to Murdo and we began the interviews of the three individuals.

The trio had gone to Montana to interview for jobs on the ski slopes. After two weeks, they had no job opportunities and not much money left so they decided to return to Florida … killing deer on their journey back. They admitted to killing five deer over a 24-hour period in Montana and Wyoming, but none in South Dakota.

Each of the men were charged with violating the Lacey Act and destruction of public property in Jackson County.

We were fortunate to uncover wildlife violations of this magnitude, all over something as juvenile as tearing a paper towel dispenser off the wall. I wish we could have thanked the truck driver for getting involved. This was one of the best 8-hour periods I ever had in my career and it was all thanks to a concerned citizen who was lucky enough to witness vandalism at a rest area.

January seems to be one of my best months for wildlife violations.

Again, in January, I received a call. It was from a friend concerning an individual who had been cited for minor violations in the past. However, all the intel I had indicated he was a deer killing machine. This particular night, the individual in question was at the bar, bragging about killing a deer the previous night.

"The game wardens don't have a clue," he boasted to everyone who would listen.

I met the Mellette County Sheriff the next day. After checking the site of the kill, we went out to the braggart's house for a visit. It was about 20 below zero, with a nice 20-mile-per-hour wind when I knocked at the door and asked him to walk with me to my truck. He wasn't dressed very warm, so I let down the tailgate and asked him to have a seat so we could visit.

I told him I knew he killed a deer two nights ago and that I had taken photos of the kill site, along with photos of the tire tracks, which matched his pickup. I went ahead and asked him to get the remains of the deer.

He did.

He admitted to killing this deer and one other deer we didn't even know about. I'm not sure if it was my interviewing skills or the balmy weather (20 below zero!), but it worked.

Tom Beck and I were working the deer decoy along with some Rosebud Tribal Wardens in Mellette County when a pickup pulled up. It stopped; a rifle rested on the window and a shot was fired.

I pulled up to the vehicle and approached the driver, asking for his driver's license and hunting license. He had neither. I cited him for shooting from a motor vehicle and attempting to take a big game animal without a license, and seized his firearm.

About a month later the Mellette County Sheriff, Junior, called and asked if I could return the .22 magnum rifle to the individual. I stated to Junior that he had not paid his fine.

"I have the cash in hand," Junior said.

Amazed, I headed down to White River with the rifle. The individual thanked me for returning his rifle, so he could continue to feed his family. I told him I was sure we would meet again!

Whenever I had an injured deer that could be salvaged, I would give it away to people who needed it in Mellette County. I'm guessing in an average year I was able to give away about 50 deer in this way. It's a win-win when animals don't go to waste and people don't have to break the law to feed their families.

One afternoon on the Bad River, I was parked on a hill overlooking the Knox Ranch. The owner and I were drinking coffee and eating cookies before I headed to a road check in Stanley County. We watched a pickup stop near two mule deer bucks standing 50 yards off the road. Three shots later, the bucks were lying on the ground. Chris and I put the coffee and cookies down and drove over to visit with the two hunters. The pair were charged with trespass, shooting from the road and hunting in the wrong unit.

Sometimes coffee and cookies are the best approach to finding wildlife violators.

Another day, another decoy operation in Mellette County.

Mick Muck, Jack Kuhl and I set up a decoy on a ranch in western Mellette County. I had been having issues with road hunters and trespassing in the area. It was the last day of deer season; it was cold and snowy. Only a few vehicles were driving past the deer decoys and we had no violations. I received a call from Mick asking if I could walk down to the road to meet the landowner.

Roger, his wife and their kids were headed to church, but she had fresh-baked caramel rolls and a thermos of coffee for me.

I can't say enough about how important those relationships and friendships were with the landowners and how much I appreciated the opportunity to serve them as a conservation officer.

Curiosity: the Game Warden's Best Friend

Dan Limmer graduated from Dakota State University with a bachelor's degree in biology and chemistry minor. He began his career with South Dakota Game, Fish & Parks in 1976 as a trapper. After he became a conservation officer, he worked in Vermillion and later in Kingsbury County.

"I wanted to be a conservation officer (CO) from the time I was 12-years-old," said Dan. He made that dream a reality in 1977 when a CO position became available in Vermillion. After a short time in Vermillion, he moved up to Kingsbury County where he remained until 1989. That year, he moved to Pierre where he worked as a senior wetland habitat biologist until 1992.

At that time, Dan moved north and spent eight years working for the National Wildlife Federation before returning to a farm in Hamlin County, South Dakota. Today, he raises native prairie grasses for seed on 300 acres near Lake Norden.

Through all these experiences though, his time as a conservation officer stands out for Dan.

"It was high stress, there were unpaid hours, it was sometimes difficult for the family," he said. "But it was an absolutely fantastic job. You had freedom, you were doing what you loved to do and you have all these experiences."

In addition to his time in the field, Dan was a firearms and defensive tactics instructor for 15 years.

"It can be really dangerous out there," said Dan. "You're usually all by yourself. I'm glad they have body cameras now – I wish we would have had them when I was on. Credibility is critical and you have to be prepared for anything."

Sometimes, that means simply paying attention to what's happening around you.

"Owen Meadows used to come work deer season with me," recalls Dan. "Kingsbury County is around where he grew up. We were parked up on a hill in the dark, having coffee and looking for lights when I heard a vehicle approaching."

In blackout mode, they were pretty well invisible in the dark. Dan pulled up and over to the shoulder. Almost before he'd even come to a stop, the approaching vehicle screamed by.

"I would say they were doing 70 miles per hour, maybe more," said Dan. "It missed us by barely a foot. If we had not heard and moved, we would have been smoked. The point is, there are a lot of ways being a conservation officer can be dangerous."

That wasn't the only time Dan was faced with the realities of the potential hazards of the job he loved.

"I was a baby game warden," he recalls. "I had just started in Vermillion after being a trapper and Ron Catlin was my training officer."

They got a tip that somebody was running a gill net at the mouth of the Vermillion River, where it dumps into the Missouri.

"I think Ron was humoring me when he agreed to the stakeout," said Dan with a chuckle. "But we got permission to use a small boat with an outboard on it. We went out and waited in the dark."

The plan was for Ron to run the motor and Dan had the light at the front. Soon, they found what they were looking for: a couple guys standing in their boat running a gill net.

"It was time to start the motor and surprise the gill netters!" said Dan. "With the first jerk, the motor doesn't start... So, Ron opened up the throttle and jerks again. The boat roared to life at full throttle! We came up so fast we almost cut that boat in half!"

The perpetrators were both from North Sioux city and had long criminal records.

"They were convicted," said Dan. "After court, one of the guys walks up to me and says 'you know, if we'd had a gun, it would have been a different story.'

Two years later, that guy went missing. Eventually, his body was found – he had been murdered. We were clearly dealing with dangerous people and we didn't even know it."

Of course, not every case was wrought with danger, but one did cost Dan a relationship.

"There was a guy I used to drink coffee with quite often," he remembers. "He was a very well-liked guy around town and I was no exception – I liked him too."

At this time in Dan's career, part of a game warden's duties included picking up road kill and disposing of it.

"Kingsbury County had a rendering plant, so that's where I took it," said Dan. "Sometimes I would stop at the plant just to see what people were throwing away. Curiosity, you know – you just never know what you might find. That particular day, I noticed a couple big black plastic bags. Next to them are two deer carcasses, tags attached. I opened the bags and inside are two deer hides. It was very atypical to throw away hides – they are usually worth money."

Dan checked out the tags – both archery. The archery season was open at the time, but one of the hides appeared to have a bullet hole through the neck.

"I laid the hides down on the carcasses," said Dan. "The bullet hole fit like a puzzle piece."

Of course, the names were on the tags. Dan knew who they were, so he went and found the guy to ask what was going on.

"He wouldn't come clean," said Dan. "So we investigated. The son was involved and he wouldn't come clean either. But I had the evidence."

At the time, Dr. Brad Randall was the South Dakota State Pathologist. Working with his boss, Dan Plut, Dan made arrangements to take the carcass and hide to Sioux Valley Hospital for an autopsy.

"The nurses were not happy to see me marching through their hall-way with a deer carcass!" said Dan. "It worked though. Randall put together a series of tests and assessments on deer carcasses so we could prove the difference between a slug hole and a broadhead hole."

These efforts also afforded Dan and his investigation an expert witness.

"The father and son simply would not fess up," said Dan. "So, the case went to jury trial. He represented himself."

The evidence held up, though Dan had to haul the carcass into the courtroom in black bags at one point.

The man was convicted and sentenced to three days in jail. He also had to pay fines and lost his hunting privileges.

"The son let his dad take the fall," said Dan. "It was sad."

One Sunday soon after, Dan and his family were in church.

"Right in front of us were some friends of this guy. When we sat down, they got up and moved to another pew. It wasn't uncommon for me to experience stuff like this, but it was difficult for my family."

Two years later, the guy finally spoke to Dan again.

"He didn't come right out and confess," remembers Dan, "but, in his own way, he told me what he needed to. It was tough to see that relationship crumble. It was harder to have my family treated badly in the community. But it was the right thing to do. It's a testimony to our commitment and perseverance in protecting the resource – that's why we do this job."

While commitment to protecting the wildlife resources of his state and county were important to Dan, it was often good old-fashioned curiosity that helped him make cases.

"I would make periodic visits to the rendering plant – you never know what people are throwing away," said Dan. "Under bridges is another great spot to just go look and see what you might see."

Dan also did a lot of night work, curiosity leading the way.

"I would leave the yard black, with all my lights out and would return that way," he said. "Especially in the fall and winter when there was snow on the ground. One particular year, there was a story around town about some 'extra-curricular activities' between two married people (they were not married to each other)."

As Dan patrolled the area, he noticed a car in the church parking lot. It was mighty late for church, so he followed his curiosity and went to take a look.

The car was unlocked and there was a purse on the seat.

"I opened the purse for identification, but there's no sign of this lady. The rumor is that she's having an affair, so I let well enough alone and continue on my way."

A few miles down the road, Dan turns onto a section line road.

"Wouldn't you know, I found another car!" said Dan. "I recognized it right away as belonging to the man involved with the rumor. Of course, I went to take a look."

As Dan approached the car, he could see from the moonlit snow that the windows were totally steamed over and the car was moving ever-so-slightly.

"I walked up to the driver's side and leaned against the car to provide some resistance," he recalls. "The movement stopped."

Giggling quietly, he backed out and left just as he'd come, in black-out mode.

"I don't think they ever knew who it was, but I suspect they spent some really nervous time that night," says Dan with a chuckle.

Curiosity generally helped make cases, however.

"Arden Petersen, a partner game warden from the neighboring county was riding with me one day," said Dan. "It was raining and we pulled up behind a car going really slowly on a gravel road."

Finally, it stopped.

"We're curious, so we're going to go visit," said Dan. "I looked at Arden as we were getting out of the truck and said 'you never know.'"

After visiting with the individuals in the car, Dan and Arden eventually got into the trunk. There, they found a shovel and the remains of a poached deer.

"They were going to bury the evidence but it was raining," said Dan. "They were sitting there waiting for the rain to stop. Our curiosity led to search warrant."

Curiosity doesn't always pay off so quickly though.

"I had a deer case that took me seven years," recalls Dan. "There was a local bar that had an annual chislic feed... but the hosts bragged about poaching whitetail deer to make it happen."

After years of patience and investigation, Dan got a call about some deer hanging in an abandoned barn.

"Abandoned or not, that barn was owned by someone," said Dan. "So, Emmett Keiser and I went and sat on it. Finally, someone came into the yard."

Two were arrested for illegal possession, but eight were charged with conspiracy.

"That pretty much shut down the old chislic feed," Dan says with a laugh. "Lots of people congratulated me on that arrest. The ring of perpetrators was not made up of the best people in town."

There were lots of good cases and lots of fun, exciting times, but being a game warden also means doing hard things sometimes.

"We were present at all the drownings in our areas," said Dan. "Stuff like that is never any fun, but pulling a kid out of the lake is awful. That's really, really tough. But it has to be done. Being a conservation officer is the best job I ever had, but some of it was not very fun."

Through the good and the bad, Dan took great pride in his work.

"I tried to be upstanding in every way," he said. "Credibility is critical anywhere you work, particularly with the states attorney. Once, I brought him a case that wasn't sure he would take, but he did. He told me 'you know, I really respect you. You have a sense of justice.' It meant an awful lot to have him say that."

For his years of service, Dan was made a life member of the South Dakota Conservation Officers Association (SDCOA).

"I'm really proud of that," he said. "It feels like the Hall of Fame! I love our reunions through the SDCOA – it's a pack of good ol' boys who shared the same work and experiences. There's a lot of the work I miss, but some of it I don't. It was a great experience, not really a job in my mind."

Last spring, Dan and Bob Brown were out hunting turkeys in Meade county. The two were trainers together during their years with SDGFP and also good friends.

"'Do you miss it?' Bob asked me.

'Yes, I do,' I replied.

'So do I.'

And that was the end of it."

Been Expecting You

By Bob Hauk

Bob Hauk began his career with South Dakota Game, Fish & Parks in 1972 as a conservation officer (CO) in Faith, South Dakota. He transferred to the Rapid City CO position in 1975. He worked in this position from 1972-1983 when he became the TIPs Coordinator. After three years in that role he became the game management supervisor for Region 1 in Rapid City. In the fall of 2000, he retired after 29 years of service to SDGFP.

One fall day, I received a call from State Police Radio reporting that a landowner south of Rapid City had called in to report a poacher on his property. He'd heard rifle shots and found a strange vehicle on his land. The guy in the vehicle would not stop, but the landowner was able to provide a vehicle description and a license plate number. As the deer season had not yet opened, I was interested.

The vehicle description was a green Ford pickup, early 1970's model. I asked State Radio to run a registration check on that license plate number. They did, but it came back on a 1980 silver Chevy suburban. Obviously, not the vehicle I was looking for.

So, I drove to State Radio and visited with the dispatcher. License plates in those days were fashioned with the county number and one letter at the beginning followed by a space and then four numbers. I was thinking the first part of the license was hard to get wrong, but perhaps the landowner may have transposed some of the last four numbers.

I began moving some of the numbers around (3486 became 3684, for example) and had the license run again. After three or four tries — bingo! – we had a 1971 green Ford pickup. It was registered to a man I knew well. I had arrested him twice for shooting deer out of season. Looked like number three was coming up.

Armed with this information and knowing where the individual lived, I headed for the address. It was dusk when I arrived. There were no lights on in the house but the 1971 green Ford pickup was sitting in the driveway.

As I walked up to the residence, I passed the vehicle in the driveway. I used my flashlight to look in the back of the pickup. There was no deer but plenty of fresh, red blood.

Although there were still no lights on in the house, I knocked on the door.

From within the house I heard a voice say, "come on in, Bob, been expecting you."

I opened the door. In the fading light, I saw the man I was looking for sitting at his kitchen table looking out the dining room windows.

After receiving an almost confessionary greeting at the door, I simply walked in, crossed the room and sat down in a chair next to him. I waited for him to speak.

Finally, he said "I knew when the landowner almost caught up to me at that gate that you would be coming."

"When we ran the vehicle plates, I knew who I was dealing with, again," I said, not mentioning the difficulty I'd had.

We had a nice, long conversation. It was very cordial and almost friendly. Sometime during that conversation, he said, "I think I am going to quit."

Not knowing for sure what he was saying or implying, I just said "good."

I finally wrote him a ticket, seized the deer that was lying on the garage floor and left.

I never thought about this conversation until many years later, but in the next 15 years of working wildlife law enforcement in this area, I never had the opportunity to visit with this man again. I never ran into him in the field or saw him at a road check. I never received a complaint call on him again and never did his name come up in any investigation I was ever involved in.

Now, I am not sure what ever really happened to this man. Maybe he died, perhaps he moved away from the area.

Or maybe, just maybe, he did quit poaching deer out of season.

Open the Trunk!

Duane Webster was a game warden in and around Custer State Park from 1968-1999. He and neighboring officer Owen Meadows, out of Fall River County, frequently assisted one another. Duane passed away in October 2013. This story is told by Owen Meadows.

Duane worked as a conservation officer in Custer Sate Park and adjacent areas. While he didn't actually supervise the young ladies at the entrance fee booths, he watched over them closely – always on the lookout for their safety and ready to dispatch any troublemakers they might encounter. Duane could come off pretty gruff, but the girls knew better – they loved him and affectionately called him "Bear."

One fall night, Duane was on patrol watching for any illicit hunting activity. Being out in the park during those hours and at time of year meant the only company he had were four legged creatures. Until, of course, he spotted something.

I was out somewhere in the southern Black Hills, also working night hunters, when Duane radioed for assistance. He had three subjects who had shot a deer and put it in the trunk of a sedan.

Duane had seen a spotlight near Blue Bell Lodge. He was able to get into position to see the deer shot and loaded. After getting the three out of the vehicle, they refused to open the trunk.

"This trunk is going to be opened one way or another," Duane told them. "You will not like the way I am going to open it."

Finally, the keys were handed over.

When Duane opened the trunk, the deer jumped out, straight into Duane's arms! Of course, no one there was giving him any help. He managed to stuff the deer back in and slam the lid. That is when the call came for assistance.

Blasting over back roads and curvy park highways can take some time, even with pursuit driving techniques. During the half hour it took me to get to him, the deer really worked over the inside of the trunk.

Upon arriving, I found out what Duane really needed help with. He wanted me to open the trunk while he would be ready to shoot the wounded deer as it leaped out.

The plan worked.

Later, Duane and I had coffee in the woods while we watched for more action and discussed the evening's excitement.

The three in the car, actually from my neck of the woods, plead guilty to several charges at their appearance in Custer County Court.

The inside of the trunk was never the same.

Henry the Hoarder

By Blair Waite

Blair Waite started his career with South Dakota Game, Fish & Parks in 1982 as an animal damage control trapper in the three most southwest counties in the state. In 2000, he became the wildlife conservation officer in Hill City, which would be his duty station until his retirement in the summer of 2014. In 2016, he began working as a seasonal ranger in Custer State Park – "a position I still have, at least for a while yet," he says, calling himself "Retired but not Tired" as of July 2018.

I met Henry M. on a warm May afternoon in 2002. I was walking up the trail on the south side of Rapid Creek above Silver City and the Pactola Reservoir. Periodically, I would observe a fisherman either dunking a worm or whipping a fly upstream. This four-mile walk-in fishery was one of the premier trout fisheries the Black Hills had to offer. And because it was also one of four "trophy trout" fisheries designated by our fishing crew, I was always extremely busy when the weather permitted. Big fish draw people.

These "trophy trout" waters were so designated because the vast majority of the rainbow trout planted there were in the 3 to 6-pound class. These four areas were in four different districts of the Black Hills. One was at Cox Lake in Lawrence County, which was patrolled by Wildlife Conservation Officer (WCO) Mike Apland, who was also one of my training officers when I began my career. Another was at Lakota Lake in Custer County, manned by my old friend Ben Chambers, WCO in Custer. The other area, besides Rapid Creek in my district, was on the downstream side of Sheridan Lake on Spring Creek. This area was the concern of both Rapid City WCOs, Chad

Sayles and Jeff Edwards. These areas demanded a lot of our attention because of the rules that governed them: only one trout over 14 inches could be kept in the daily limit of five, with a possession limit at any given time of double the daily limit.

A five-pound trout would be well over 14 inches in length, meaning large fish were plentiful in these spots. Also, because these were planted fish, raised at our trout hatcheries in Rapid City and outside of Spearfish, they were not overly hard to catch. Fly fishermen and tourists not accustomed to trout fishing got quite a thrill catching these big fish. It drew a lot of people, making it well worth the expense – approximately $25.00 – of raising a trout to that size to be released.

So, back to the day I met Henry...

About a half a mile up the trail, I encountered three people walking out with what looked like three big rainbow trout on a stringer. Two adult men and a younger teenage girl. One of them was Henry.

I didn't even get a chance to introduce myself.

"Who are you and where did you come from?" demanded Henry.

I stated my name and told them I was the game warden from Hill City. Henry immediately started name-dropping my neighboring WCO's and said he had not heard of me.

I would later find out that Henry regularly contacted our office in Rapid City and conversed with whomever he could in order to find out where the officers were on any given day. He always had "pertinent information" to give them and needed to know where they were. Good to know where your adversary was, to make the plan for the day.

After some chit chat about how fishing was, what they were using for bait and other small talk, I checked their licenses. The other adult was

Henry's brother and the young lady was Henry's daughter. I mentally made note of their names, addresses and other information. It seemed to me that something was up with this bunch … something just didn't add up with the encounter.

Several days later, I mentioned Henry's name to Ben Chambers, my neighbor to the south and Jeff Edwards in Rapid City. Both were well aware of Henry and had checked him on several occasions in their respective districts. It seemed he was always with a limit of large trout … never any small ones in their possession.

I got a lot of intel that summer when I was surveilling the walk-in fisheries above Silver City. I learned that Henry drove an old Dodge Aspen, what time he showed up to fish and that he normally left the area after dark. He always fished with his brother and his daughter, and never left until he limited out with big trout, ignoring smaller trout and never keeping any of them. In fact, he was always there when I showed up in the evening checking fishermen and limit compliances.

I wondered how anybody could eat that amount of fish. Perhaps he was feeding the neighborhood or donating much of the fish to needy people?

Most of the time, I purposely walked around Henry and his group and carefully watched his activity, not even letting him know that I had my eye on them. Henry's favorite fishing spot on Rapid Creek was on the second bridge upstream from the parking lot. This was a location where nobody could sneak up on him – he could see both ways for some distance. He used PowerBait – a commercially made bait that resembles play dough, scented to catch different fish – and took little time to catch his fish. I never caught him in any violation that summer but still had a sixth-sense feeling that something wasn't right … I just couldn't put it together.

Conversing with Ben Chambers one day, Ben mentioned he had checked Henry and his group that day at Lakota Lake with a limit of large trout. I too had seen Henry that afternoon, fishing in Rapid Creek but spent little time observing him. The creek was hopping with fishermen that day, so I did not know what was caught there or by whom.

However, the picture was now coming together. Henry wanted to know where we were at various times so he could fish in one of our areas and not be checked, then go to another area and fish, perhaps over-bagging on large trout without being checked twice in one day.

The game was afoot.

I contacted Mike Apland, Jeff Edwards, Chad Sayles and Ben Chambers; we put ourselves on alert, keeping each other informed of Henry's whereabouts. I started working Henry seriously from that day on.

In 2002 our agency had no night vision equipment. I enticed my immediate supervisor, Jim McCormick, to ask the Division of Criminal Investigation (DCI) to borrow a set of night vision glasses to use in surveillance of Henry and his nighttime activities.

Later that summer, I was 15 feet up a pine tree, clinging to a branch and waiting for Henry and his brother and daughter to come back to their vehicle. Theirs was the last car in the parking lot.

About 10:30 that evening, the approximate time Henry always came back with his fish, he appeared with his usual partners out of the total darkness. They walked within 20 feet of me and the conversation they were having is still fresh in my mind. It was very apparent they did not like game wardens. The conversation was about what they would do to us if they could, what they thought of us "SOBs" and what they thought they were getting away with.

I wanted so badly to fly out of that tree and give them their shot but thought better of it. Through the night vision glasses, I could see no violation and did not want to show that we were actively working them.

I kept notes of Henry's activities for that whole summer but had no concrete evidence of any fishing violations.

The following spring, I was called by our office's senior secretary Verma Stehly. She informed me Henry had called the office that morning asking questions about when the first fish planting was going to happen.

The fish had been planted just two days before and Verma was giving us a heads up that Henry's activities were about to start. Verma was always just "one of the boys" in resource law enforcement and helped us any way she could. All of us respected her tremendously and do to this day!

After the information from Verma, the Black Hills Wardens decided once again that we would keep a steady lookout for Henry and his crew. As of early June of 2003, Henry had already been observed at three of the four trophy trout fishing waters. And because we hypothesized that Henry was hitting different trophy waters in different wardens' districts, we were already ahead of the game from a year ago.

On a warm mid-day in June, Chad Sayles had just left Pactola Reservoir. He had been doing boat safety and fishing compliance work and was heading back to the regional office in Rapid City. He was traveling east on Sheridan Lake Road when he radioed me.

"The fox is in the hen house! The fox is in the hen house! The fox is in the hen house!" was the radio traffic I received. With a wrinkled nose and low eye brow I replied, "what in the heck are you talking about?"

Chad immediately informed me he had just passed Henry fishing on Spring Creek and his brother and daughter were with him. I asked if he had time to ditch the boat and observe him for a spell, to which he replied in the affirmative.

At that moment, I was north of Pactola Reservoir near Roubaix Lake. I asked if Chad would keep me in the know of Henry's activities. I drove south to Silver City Road and awaited Chad's report.

It didn't take long before Chad radioed me that he observed Henry catch what he thought was about a 7-pound milker trout (a brood fish that had outlived its usefulness at the hatchery). He also observed Henry's brother fishing but not catch anything and his daughter not fish at all. Chad also observed Henry converse with a fisherman who was just leaving his vehicle. He noted the license plate for future reference. Soon thereafter, Chad radioed me and stated that Henry had loaded up and was heading my way.

I immediately went to the Rapid Creek/Silver City parking lot. I hid my squad truck in the usual spot, loaded up my "possibles bag" with everything I thought I would need – a 20-power scope, portable radio, snacks and water – and proceeded to my hiding spot. I waited on the rim rock 500 yards above the second bridge. Within the hour Henry, his brother and his daughter appeared and set up to fish downstream from the bridge. His daughter took a paperback book out of a backpack and commenced to read as her dad and uncle PowerBaited up and started to fish.

Within a half hour, Henry's brother had hooked and landed a five pounder. He put it on the stringer and continued to fish. An hour later Henry hooked and landed a large rainbow trout. He also put it on the stringer… and continued to fish.

Being that this was his second large trout of the day I figured I, with the help of my fellow wardens, had finally caught Henry in a violation. I was about to walk down the steep and jagged rocks to confront Henry, when I noticed that they were picking up to leave. I immediately radioed Regional Supervisor Mike Kintigh and asked him to come in an unmarked vehicle to wait in the parking lot and observe where Henry placed the trout when he got back to his vehicle.

Shortly thereafter, I radioed my immediate supervisor Jim McCormick to wait near the fish hatchery in an unmarked vehicle on Highway 44 in Rapid City. When he encountered Henry's Dodge Aspen, he would follow it wherever it was going and discretely observe what Henry unloaded and where he put it.

For once in my life, timing was perfect.

Kintigh was in the parking lot – far enough away to be discreet, but close enough to observe Henry put the two trout in a blue cooler and see the third trout already there. Kintigh followed Henry out of the parking lot and followed the car down highway 44, where McCormick picked up the vehicle and tailed it to Henry's house. There, Jim observed Henry remove the blue cooler and bring it into his house. All this visual observation gave me the probable cause, essential in any criminal case, to write a search warrant for Henry's house. We would be able to retrieve any contraband pertaining to the fishing violation that might be found at Henry's residence.

On Monday morning I wrote the search warrant. Jim McCormick and I went to Henry's home late in the afternoon after Henry had gotten home from work. We sat on Henry's picnic table and went over the previous Saturday evening's fishing activities.

Henry contended that he had caught one fish, his brother had caught one fish and his daughter had caught one fish. When questioned where each fish had been caught, he stated that his daughter had caught the fish on Spring Creek, where Chad had observed Henry catch it and had also retrieved a written statement from the fisherman at his vehicle. The fisherman had conversed with Henry, during which time Henry admitted that he had caught the 7-pounder.

Bragging will get you every time.

When asked how many fish he had in his possession in his residence, Henry did not know but said they eat a lot of them. I asked Henry for consent search of his residence and he obliged. McCormick and I walked into the house with Henry and opened the top freezer to his kitchen refrigerator. Inside the freezer were bags of frozen rainbow trout fillets.

Given the facts that he could have gifted a possession limit of fish to his wife, (two large trout), that his daughter still lived with them and the statement Henry gave saying his brother also stored his trout there, they could have legally had eight large trout for a total possession limit in the household.

However, in that freezer alone, Henry had over 20 trout fillets, each from a 3 to 6-pound fish. At this time Henry became irate. He stated that he believed his constitutional rights were being violated and withdrew his consent to search, so I presented him with a legally signed and executed search warrant. Henry's eyes were on fire; he yelled "you got a f---ing search warrant for my house?!?"

Jim and I immediately went into de-escalation mode to calm him down.

In the basement there were three additional chest freezers. Here, we found several quarters of deer meat that were freezer burnt. There was bag after bag of fish including northerns, bullheads and crappie, as well as several domestic hams and other assorted frozen meat.

But we also found many bags of rainbow trout fillets. We took possession of the trout. Law Supervisor Bruce Nachtigal and I thawed them out and counted 369 pairs of trout fillets. We estimated that 90% of them were large, from a 3 to 6-pound fish. After some consultation, we let Henry have 50 of the fish in his possession and charged him with 319 trout over the possession limit.

During the court proceedings Henry pled guilty to all counts. He was fined $2,000 and sentenced to 319 days in jail. He had 299 days suspended and had to serve 20 days. The civil damages amounted to $31,900 and he lost his fishing privileges for one year.

Blair Waite, left front, is pictured with his fellow officers and the fish seized from "Henry the Hoarder."

Afterwards, Henry remained absent from the fishing scene in my district for many years. I never had the chance to check him fishing again until the month before I retired. I recognized his familiar face, fishing at a new pond created just south of Hill City. If he recognized me, he didn't let on.

Game, Fish & Parks eventually discontinued trophy trout fishing, as the temptation to overbag was just too overwhelming for some. However, trout fishing is still big in the Black Hills – especially fly fishing.

Through the cooperation and friendship of my fellow wardens, supervisors and regional office secretary, we made a good case. In fact, it is South Dakota's largest ever trout overbag case, as far as I am aware.

This case could not have been made if only a single component had failed. This was an outstanding example of working relationships and dedication to preserving our wildlife and fisheries. Officers, supervisors and office personnel worked in harmony; everyone knew what was happening and everyone wanted it stopped. This case was really a credit to teamwork.

I'd Prefer a Camel

By Owen Meadows

Owen spent his career as a conservation officer in Hot Springs. He served as a state game warden and then a conservation officer from 1967-2000. Owen was a founding member of the South Dakota Conservation Officers Association (SDCOA) and also served on the board in various capacities.

In early January 1991, a rancher located in the far northeast part of Fall River County called. He was wondering if I could stop out at the ranch and pick up a dead a bald eagle he had found.

In route to his ranch, he called and advised that he would meet me along the way so I could pick up the eagle.

After meeting and visiting a bit, I took the eagle out of his pickup to examine it on the county road. The eagle had a noticeable bulge on its neck. Knowing that there are times when eagles gorge while eating a critter, I decided to cut the neck open to expose the contents.

This is the point when my knowledge of eagle deaths seemed to fade... As officers of Game, Fish and Parks, we had been warned to be cautious of any raptor or predator deaths we might come across because of several animal poisoning events that had occurred in the western states.

But was I remembering this at the time? No.

So, there I was, ready to cut the neck open to see what there might be that killed the eagle. Of course, being curious and not really very cautious, I cut the neck area open without wearing any rubber gloves.

As soon as the lump was exposed, I thought, "you dumb ass Owen, this is probably a poison-laden fat ball used to kill any predator..."

I thanked the rancher, placed the eagle in the pickup box and drove away.

After approximately a mile or so, I got a feeling... a feeling like I might have brushed my lip with my hand (you understand the feeling I am referring to – you might get it when you pick up after your dog or after you have used the great outdoors as a bathroom). I pulled over to wash my hands and face in the snow along the road. After getting that accomplished, I headed out again.

Within a half mile, I had a feeling from my toes to the top of my head as though I had taken a long drag from a Camel straight cigarette, two inches in diameter.

Cussing Owen again, I radioed dispatch to advise of my location and direction of travel. In case check out time was near, I wanted the Buffalo Gap ambulance service to know where I was.

Soon, I experienced another Camel-straight-like feeling. About that time a rancher and ambulance service member radioed. He said that by the time he would get to the ambulance shed, I should be there also. If not, he was planning to head east along my intended route to meet me.

His estimate of arrival was correct. He ordered that to save time we were continuing to Hot Springs with him driving and using the pickup's radio, lights and siren. Periodically during the ride to the hospital, the Camel-straight-like feeling would come and go, but seemed to be lessening just a bit.

When we arrived at the emergency room, the doctor had already received some information about the situation relayed by radio.

"I hear you believe you have come in contact with poison," she said. "What is it?"

I had no idea and could only relate the Camel straight feeling. Unsure of treatment, the doctor continued monitoring vitals. The symptoms continued to lessen as two or three hours passed. They let me go and I seemed to feel fairly well. No prosecution occurred due to the lack of information pointing to any specific area where the eagle came across the fat ball.

Later, lab results determined the fat ball contained an agricultural pesticide called Temik. It is a pre-emergent granule which becomes absorbed by a plant, then kills any insect that might take a bite.

One granule of Temik, about the size of three grains of pepper, will kill a robin. I heard a story of a lady who thought Temik might be a good treatment for her potted roses. When she nibbled on a shoot of spearmint growing in the pot, she became very ill and was treated with atropine sulfate (an antidote for nerve agents).

Temik acts on acetyl cholinesterase, an enzyme that facilitates the signals at the nerve endings. Uncontrolled movement, paralysis and death occur if the exposure to Temik is sufficient.

Temik is a carbamate rather than an organophosphate. Carbamates are short-lived when ingested at low levels and passed through urine within six hours. On the other hand, organophosphates are more stubborn, lasting weeks.

Better to experience a carbamate than the organophosphate, but I still prefer a Camel.

Perhaps Not the First Female Game Warden, but Definitely Not the Last

Mary Clawson began her career with South Dakota Game, Fish & Parks in June, 1986. She spent 14 years as conservation officer, first in Pickstown/Lake Andes and later in Aberdeen. In March of 2000 she was promoted to regional habitat manager, which allowed her to maintain her law enforcement certification. In 2006 she retired from law enforcement but remained regional habitat manager. She retired fully in February 2012.

"I grew up in Indiana," said Mary. "I earned my bachelor's degree at Purdue University and my master's at the University of Missouri, Columbia. Both are in Wildlife and Fisheries Management. I didn't necessarily intend to work in wildlife law enforcement, but when the opportunity came, I was ready for the challenge."

Mary's first job was with US Fish & Wildlife Service on the Iowa/Nebraska border, at DeSoto National Wildlife Refuge. There, she met the man who would become her husband. He took a transfer that brought them to South Dakota.

"When we moved to South Dakota, our two girls weren't so little anymore and I was ready to start working on my career again," recalls Mary. "There was an opening for a wildlife conservation officer (WCO) in Lake Andes, so I decided to apply."

Of course, there were rumors and rumblings about a WOMAN wanting to be an officer. It seemed very few women had ever applied.

"I'm not sure everyone was quite ready to have a woman on the force," said Mary. "But my qualifications were good, my education was good and I could drive on the snow and ice. They hired me."

Shortly after she started, however, she learned she was not truly the first female "game warden" to work in South Dakota.

"I got a letter from a lady named Caryll Hawley Bognoski in Council Bluffs, Iowa," Mary recalls. "It said 'you are not the first lady game warden, I was.'"

Mary learned that Caryll Hawley was a young woman in the 1920's, around the time the Game Lodge was first built in Custer State Park. Caryll's father was the chief game warden in South Dakota at the time.

"They had deputy game wardens designated in each county," Mary recalls. "They would enforce what laws there were and take people to the justice of the peace for their court appearance. At that time, the arresting warden received a portion of the fine."

Mary met Caryll in person at her house in Council Bluffs. "Caryll told me that she spent two summers at Custer State Park, selling fishing licenses," said Mary. "She met General Custer's widow, Mary, and later received a letter from her. Caryll also recalled seeing President Calvin Coolidge, who liked to come out to Custer State Park and stay at the Game Lodge.

"It was inspiring to hear about the history of wildlife law enforcement in our state and to meet this wonderful lady!" said Mary. "I always intended to work in habitat management, but wildlife law enforcement is every bit as important. If you don't regulate the harvest, you've got nothing to manage. Caryll Hawley was right there at the beginning of those efforts in South Dakota."

Mary loved the diversity that came with working as a game warden and took advantage of as many learning opportunities as she could.

"I really enjoyed all parts of the job," she said. "Every day was different and every season of the year brought different duties. I really enjoyed getting to know 'my' county and the game production areas I managed, the landowners who managed their private land, and the hunters and anglers I would encounter who were utilizing the resources I sought to manage and protect."

Mary also enjoyed the 'other duties' and opportunities she was able to take part in over the years, like walleye spawning on the Missouri River in the spring, which sometimes included white caps on the river or snow and ice. She worked the Sturgis Rally with the South Dakota Highway Patrol officers. Mary was one of the actors in a video about using non-toxic shot with Tom Roster. She trapped and tagged deer in Gregory County with WCO Denny Lengkeek for a movement study and trapped pheasants from the Lake Andes National Wildlife Refuge to be transplanted in Edmunds, McPherson and Fall River Counties.

"I was also involved with NAWEOA," said Mary. "That's the North American Wildlife Enforcement Officers Association. I attended conferences in the United States and Canada, and served on their board as Region 6 Director, which is the Midwestern US. That organization was a game changer for me."

In particular, NAWEOA helped Mary meet other female wardens.

"Two of the women I met at my first conference in Wyoming are still some of my dearest friends," she said. "It was nice to have other women to talk over the challenges of the job and how they coped. Most of the guys I worked with were great and very welcoming, but their experiences were just not the same. Having said that, I would never have survived the job without the support and encouragement of many of my co-workers, especially my 'unofficial field training officer' Denny Lengkeek."

Today, when a new WCO is hired by South Dakota Game, Fish & Parks, they are sent to the Law Enforcement Academy in Pierre.

After successful completion of that training, they spend 12 weeks in the field working alongside designated field training officers – WCOs who have been doing the work for a number of years.

When Mary was hired, there were no field training officers – this part of the training process had yet to be developed.

"We were given a ticket book, the law book, a pickup truck and some forms to fill out as needed," recalls Mary. "Then, we were sent to our duty station to get to know the area. Denny was my neighbor to the west; he very graciously answered all of my questions and helped me learn how to become a game warden. Not very many years later, the department decided to create a field training program for newly minted game wardens, which I wholeheartedly endorsed."

Mary's family – like every other law enforcement family – had to be flexible and knew she might get called out at any time.

"My husband was an assistant refuge manager and his days were typically 8-4:30," recalls Mary. "Of course, I worked a lot of weekends, so Dad was home with the girls. But we still had to juggle his travels for work and his refuge law enforcement duties."

Mary described one definite downside to being the "lady game warden" – gossip and rumors. Within a year of being hired, various rumors started circulating in Charles Mix County about Mary – ALL of them FALSE. There was a rumor that she was thrown into the lake (Lake Andes) or the reservoir (Francis Case). Another story detailed a fictitious assault in which had her gun taken away by an attacker. Last, but certainly not least, was the rumor that she'd actually been killed.

When Mary moved to Aberdeen (Brown County), she had hoped that these rumors would be left behind...but that was not to be.

"Some of the kids in the high school my girls attended decided to tell them their mother was assaulted, with all the gory details. Of course they denied this, because it never happened," she remembers. "I hadn't ever told my girls about this rumor – it never occurred to me that they would hear it from their peers, who heard it from their parents, because it was not true. Stories like this tend to plague female officers in every branch of law enforcement and, unfortunately, it seems to come up every few years. All the stories remain untrue."

Despite the challenges of being a conservation officer, as well as the added challenges of being a female officer, Mary loved her work.

"I would never have guessed that I would work in law enforcement, but I would not change anything," she said. "I think being a game warden was wonderful!"

One case in particular stands out as a point of pride.

"I was contacted by a warden from Arizona about an Aberdeen local who had hunted elk and javelina illegally down there," Mary recalls. "I wrote and executed a search warrant on the guy's house. We collected evidence for Arizona where he was successfully prosecuted, along with additional evidence that included video of another illegal hunt."

Mary forwarded the incriminating video to the US Fish & Wildlife Service Special Agents in Wyoming and the man was charged with Lacey Act violations for the illegal taking of a moose. His trophy mount of the animal was seized.

It was moments like these during her career that ignited her passion to protect and preserve wildlife and environmental resources.

"We've got to leave the land as good or better than we found it," she said, "and that includes wildlife. We must have sustainable harvests to balance the needs of the people and the wildlife. We need people who don't want to see our wildlife heritage destroyed by greed and politics – that means men and women, hunters, hikers, photographers, everyone."

Mary is proud of the work she did.

"I think I did a really good job. I'll say it and put myself up there with any of the guys I worked with. Women as game wardens bring a unique set of qualities that help us perform the job. It's not all about muscles and brawn. It's a mental game. You need to be intelligent and observant, have conversation skills, time management skills and good rapport with people. Of course, none of these things are gender specific. But I think women tend to be a little more collaborative, which is well suited to the job at hand. I think I rose to the challenge and succeeded."

Wives Do Not Lie

By Bob Hauk

Bob Hauk began his career with South Dakota Game, Fish & Parks in 1972 as a conservation officer (CO) in Faith, South Dakota. He transferred to the Rapid City CO position in 1975. He worked in this position from 1972-1983 when he became the TIPs Coordinator. After three years in that role he became the game management supervisor for Region 1 in Rapid City. In the fall of 2000, he retired after 29 years of service to SDGFP.

Late one afternoon around 4 p.m., several conservation officers and myself were conducting a November road check for Black Hills deer hunters. A pickup came through the check with three hunters in the vehicle and a small whitetail buck in the back.

The deer was tagged and everything appeared okay until I tried to read the name on the tag… the name did not belong to any of the hunters.

"Whose deer is this?" I asked.

After lots of shuffling around one of the hunters finally spoke up.

"It belongs to my wife," he said.

Apparently, she had been along earlier in the day, shot the buck and had gone home in another vehicle around noon. I asked for his telephone number and told him I would call and check things out.

I left him in his vehicle and returned to mine.

I called State Police Radio (this was before we had cell phones – only rich people in the movies had a telephone in a vehicle). I asked the dispatcher to call the number and ask the lady if she had indeed gone hunting that day. If she did was she successful? If so, did she shoot a doe or a buck? If it was a buck how many points did it have?

"Okay," he said, "I will get back to you."

About 10 minutes later he called me back on the radio and said he had tried several times but nobody was answering at that number.

"Thanks," I said. "I will go back and talk to the hunter."

On the way back to the vehicle, I decided to change my tactics. Instead of giving him the information I already knew, I would ask him for a response first.

"Sir, you will have to come with me," I told him. "Wives just don't lie about these things, do they?"

"I knew she would not lie," he said, climbing out of his pickup. "She is too good of a person for that. I killed the buck and put her tag on it."

I walked him back to my pickup never mentioning the telephone call. I wrote him a ticket, confiscated the deer and sent him on his way.

But I have always wondered what the conversation was like at his house that evening…

He knew he had already confessed to shooting an illegal deer to a game warden, had the deer confiscated and gotten a ticket. Then his wife must have said, "what phone call? I was not even home around 4 p.m.!"

Or maybe he was thinking about the last piece of information I left him with.

"If you cooperate, we can leave your wife out of this and not charge her with lending a license to another."

For this he was very grateful and thanked me for my consideration.

The Many Hats Worn by the Conservation Officer

Michael Yost began his career with South Dakota Game, Fish & Parks working on a fisheries-land crew out of Sioux Falls before he transferred to Webster for a fisheries position. He started as a conservation officer for Faulk County in the mid-1980's and transferred to Spink County in the early 1990s. Both Spink and Faulk Counties became his duty station. Michael retired in 2007 with 27 years of service with Game, Fish and Parks and went to work as a code enforcement officer for the City of Redfield and Spink County. When he's not working, he spends time on his farm in Faulk County, planting trees, improving habitat and filming wildlife.

"The part of my job I loved the most other than wildlife was working with kids," said Michael Yost. "But, as a conservation officer, I really got a taste of just about everything."

Conservation officers in South Dakota are fully certified law enforcement officers. They receive training at the Law Enforcement Academy in Pierre, qualify with their firearms annually and receive continuing training to maintain their certifications.

This is on top of their wildlife duties that include biological surveys, aerial winter deer detail, dealing with injured or displaced animals and conservation efforts. Educator, writer, photographer, first responder and local contact for all things wildlife add to the list.

But, as Michael said, working with youth and helping others learn to love the outdoors was something he was – and still is – truly passionate about.

"Over the years, as a conservation officer and after my retirement, I hosted some outdoor classroom events," he said. "I had schools come to our land in Faulk County or to wildlife areas for field trips. I worked with staff in our area from National Resources Conservation Services (NRCS), which is a federal agency, and Pheasants Forever. I talked to the kids about conservation practices for habitat, including grasses, trees and water projects. The other two gave presentations about rangeland, native grasses and soil conservation."

Michael was very glad to have schools on board with the effort and gave back to the school district by serving as an assistant wrestling, baseball and weightlifting coach for many years in Redfield. He also gave presentations to civic groups and assisted living centers, along with the Developmental Center located in town.

"Educating people was important to me," he said. "I created the 'Outdoor View' newspaper column to go in the *Faulk County Record* and the *Redfield Press* and put weekly information out. The public seemed to enjoy it!"

One year, South Dakota was celebrating the 'pheasantennial.'

"We took the opportunity to visit with the kids about Spink County and the first pheasant releases in South Dakota," Michael said. "We got some history in along with all the other topics! Also, I enjoyed doing the Hunt Safe presentations and a variety of game calls at the end of my talks. The kids and parents always laughed – it was a lot of fun!"

During his years as a game warden, Michael had several cases that stood out. One case in particular involved a TIPs call, Michael's brother Martin who was also a conservation officer and over 400 illegally taken fish.

"I received information through the TIPs program with a call coming directly from an informant," said Michael. "I called my brother Martin and he went to the lake I told him about because it was closer to his area. He watched the group in question. Martin saw them fishing and then some people left the lake with fish in a large cooler. We suspected it was full of large perch."

Martin had identified the individuals and knew they were from a nearby town in Spink County. He called Michael and asked him to go have a look around the community.

"This community was not large," said Michael. "It was about my second sweep through town when I noticed a garage door open – about two feet is all – with lights on inside."

Michael pulled over and got out of his truck. He could hear voices in the garage.

"As I walked to the door, I heard the sound of electric fillet knives and talk about perch."

Michael banged on the door.

"Hey guys, are you cleaning some fish in there?"

"Yes we are!" came the answer. "We have some nice perch!"

"State game warden," Michael replied. "I'd like to come in and have a look."

"Ok… come in," they said.

Michael went in and confirmed the suspicions that the group was over their limit on perch.

"They were over their limit with what they had in the freezer as well," recalls Michael. "We found walleye that were so freezer burnt you couldn't eat them."

In the end, the guilty parties wrote a letter to Pierre saying Michael and Martin had been too rough on them and complaining that they never caught fish every day.

"They seemed to think that, because they had days when they didn't catch any fish, they should be allowed to catch their limit and then some," said Michael. "They felt entitled."

Whatever their motivation to break the law, it was a good case that resulted in the arrest of five individuals. They paid over $600 in fines and lost their fishing privileges for two years. A photo of Michael and his brother Martin, along with the 478 seized perch, appeared on the back cover of the 2001 South Dakota Fishing Handbook.

"It was one in a million case really," said Michael. "For us to be together as brothers and game wardens for South Dakota made it even better."

Another good fish case came from some undercover work Michael was doing.

"We watched fishermen in another boat take too many walleyes," said Michael. "As they caught fish, they would 'high grade' them, meaning they would keep the bigger fish and throw out smaller fish they'd already caught, which were already dead."

When the fishermen that were illegally taking fish came out of some flooded trees, Michael and his assistant in the unmarked boat made their way over to them.

"I hollered over and asked if they had any extra fish because we weren't having good luck," recalls Michael. "They said 'sure' and brought us some over."

After they had passed the fish over, Michael showed them his game warden badge and informed them he was coming aboard their boat for an inspection.

"I'll never forget what one guy said – 'you've got to be kidding me!'" said Michael. "But I was not kidding. There was other language used too, but you get the idea!"

Michael ended up seizing all the perch and walleyes they had taken, as well as collecting bond money and giving tickets for fish over their limit. He also gave them a warning citation for a life jacket violation.

"They were out-of-state fishermen," he recalls. "They were good about it though. I was polite with them and they apologized repeatedly, saying they were just trying to help give fish to other boaters on the lake."

Unfortunately, their good will didn't make it legal.

"As a game warden, sometimes I would act like I agreed with the violator's excuses so they could leave my company and think they had a good reason why they got a ticket," said Michael. "I never gave tickets and chewed on them at the same time. My states attorneys – I had two counties in my duty station – both told me to settle it in the field and not in court if possible. So, when in doubt, I was always polite and firm as long as everyone was safe."

Like many conservation officers, Michael's passion for his job sometimes made it difficult to ignore violations even when he wasn't working.

"If I was off duty (which was never, it seemed), I would write tickets to those I felt were pretty obvious about violating game or fish laws," said Michael. "My supervisor told me once to just look the other way when I was out for fun, but I just couldn't. People know who you are most of the time and I felt I had to set an example. Many times, I wrote tickets when my dad, my wife or my sons were with me for things like over-bagging on fish limits or too many fishing lines out. Maybe it's another example of undercover work? I only did this when it was safe for those with me. I almost hated to go camping in public areas because of the wildlife and fish violations I would inevitably see, but I always had my ticket book and game warden ID with me."

It wasn't just fish that kept Michael busy concerning wildlife violations, though.

"One year, we had an eagle shot in our area," recalls Michael. "The guy claimed he shot it out of the air."

During the interview, the culprit claimed he thought the bird was a crow or hawk. He dug himself in a little deeper by answering in the affirmative when Michael asked if he'd shot hawks before.

"A picture of me holding the poached bald eagle from that case was printed on the cover of the TIPs brochure in 2007, when I retired," said Michael. "It was a great way to retire, I thought, with that honor!"

Michael Yost is pictured on the TIPs brochure
with a poached bald eagle.

The guilty party received a very large fine and lost his hunting privileges for five years in that bald eagle case.

Over the course of his career, Michael dealt with more than eight eagles, bald and golden, shot in Faulk and Spink Counties.

"If they were alive, I transported the eagles to Pierre, Watertown or Huron to zoos or other facilities that could x-ray and maybe save them," said Michael. "Sometimes they did not make it, which was a really sad deal. Also, I saw owls and hawks of many species that had been shot or otherwise injured. Not to mention every waterfowl and bird you can think of... I've had them in my hands with a decision to make. I have such compassion for wildlife, I just hated dealing with hurt animals. Sometimes you have to euthanize or put them down, but when people bring you a wounded animal, they are really trusting you to deal with it in the best way you can."

Deer are the primary big game in Spink and Faulk Counties, and Michael dealt with violations concerning deer as well.

"This case came from another TIPs call," he said. "However, what stood out to me was the way other agencies worked together to see it through."

The Faulk County Sheriff received a TIPs call about several people hunting deer and not tagging them. The sheriff met up with Michael and the two went to investigate in the sheriff's vehicle.

When they arrived in the area indicated by the TIPs information, they followed a Chevy Blazer for a while. They watched the vehicle go into a farmyard and unload two deer.

When the Blazer left, Michael and the sheriff went down the driveway to the garage where the Blazer had unloaded the two deer. One of the two garage doors was open. Through the door, from the outside, they could see four deer hanging, in addition to the two other deer that had been unloaded outside. None of the deer were tagged.

"We waited for the Blazer to return," said Michael. "When it did, it slowed down but then continued past the driveway entrance. We pursued and stopped them."

The Blazer contained another untagged deer that had not yet been field dressed. After visiting with the occupants of the Blazer, the officers and the hunters returned to the farmyard where they met another vehicle.

"The sheriff went back to town to get my truck at that point," recalls Michael. "I stayed and began interviewing each member of the group – a total of seven hunters."

As the story unfolded, another deputy was called to assist with security and collecting evidence.

"In the end, there were seven counts of transporting untagged deer," said Michael. "It was a good case for Faulk County and an excellent example of agencies working together. I was always very appreciative of the good relationships I had with law enforcement officers and other agencies around me. We worked together on just about everything that needed to be done."

Michael also frequently worked with the previous manager of Fisher Grove State Park, another Game, Fish & Parks employee.

"Dan Grewing was his name. He helped me with a lot of different things and I helped him," said Michael. "One time, I had a call about a deer out on the ice – thin ice, of course – and it couldn't get off of Cottonwood Lake in Spink County."

After consulting Dan about the problem, the pair decided to take out an old flat bottom boat that had ice breakers on it.

"I had a mallet up in front of boat and Dan was in the back running the gas motor," said Michael. "We were testing ice thickness with the mallet and busting our way out to this deer. We managed to get a rope on it and drag it out. It was just fine and ran away after we got it off the ice!"

There were a good number of folks watching, as Michael recalls.

"Luckily we got the deer off ok," he said. "It was good public relations, we were told."

Many other animals-in-distress calls or people-in-distress-because-of-an-animal calls came to Michael over the years. One in particular that people didn't want to handle themselves was snapping turtles.

"I had many snapping turtle calls," said Michael. "With the local Turtle Creek water coming through Redfield Lake and the James River nearby, we had lots around. Snapping turtles do really well in these waters. They would be in garbage cans, on roads near homes or on local streets in the springtime. They were moving slowly, of course, but no one really wanted to touch or move them closer to water. So I got the call."

During lake surveys, snapping turtles would frequently get caught in the frame nets.

"They are difficult to get out of nets," said Michael. "Their claws hook into the netting when you pull them out by their tail. They will definitely scratch and bite you if you're not careful. Once, I scared a local guy who was helping me with the nets in the boat. I got the turtle out of the net and put it into the flat bottom boat. While he was looking away for a second, I grabbed his calf and hissed (snappers hiss a lot) and he about jumped out of the boat! Thought the turtle bit him. Funny for me, but he didn't really think so. We laughed about it later."

In addition to wandering snapping turtles, there were calls about deer and rabbits eating trees, shrubs and flowers in town.

"I also had many calls about wood ducks and their little ones. My wife and sons would sometimes help chase the baby ducks in town.

We tried to capture the whole brood and the mom duck too, if we could. I used dip nets, fishing seines and garbage cans to capture wildlife that needed to leave town or move on. I had lots of calls from the public on these issues during my career."

As conservation officers, Michael and his fellow officers worked to protect wildlife and to serve the public. Sometimes, situations come up in the public where people need help instead of wildlife. Of course, conservation officers jump right in when they are needed.

"There were several drownings that I worked on from boats and shorelines," recalls Michael. "I also helped deal with the fatal helicopter crash that took place in Spink County. They were all emotional and hard to deal with. I worked with other agencies on these tragedies and still think back to those days sometimes. We did not get to visit with anyone back then about how we felt regarding being involved in these tragedies – you just did the work. Looking back, it might have helped to talk to someone, I guess."

It wasn't all tragedy though.

"One day, several of us game wardens were eating in a café in Turton, which is a tiny town in Spink County," recalls Michael. "It was mid-afternoon during the opening day of pheasant season many years ago. Some officers were done eating and had left the café. I was finishing lunch with another game warden when someone yelled 'he's having a heart attack!'"

'Here we go,' thought Michael, looking Arlo Haase, the game warden sitting next to him.

Michael went to the man lying on the floor.

"He was just mumbling and unresponsive," said Michael. "He was breathing, however. The lady with him said he had a heart condition and we yelled for someone to call an ambulance. Turton is a small town a long way from any facilities."

Michael started chest compressions while Arlo cleared the area around him on the floor and made sure the man was still breathing.

"In the end, the fella lived," said Michael. "But he did have some broken ribs from chest compressions I gave him. When the ambulance showed up, they gave him oxygen and handled it from there. I admit I was very nervous – it was my first time with something like that."

The *Aberdeen American News* printed an article about the event in the tiny community.

"The article talked about how we saved the guy's life and said people should look at conservation officers as helpers – we were good guys. That day made me feel proud to be a game warden, along with many other things I did in the course of my career. I was glad the department trained us to help in situations like these with all the CPR, first aid and other training we received. I'm also very grateful to my wife Leda and our sons Parker and Ryan for helping me with the job!"

Like any job, Michael admits there were days when he wondered if he would do it again.

"Yes," he knows now. "Yes I would."

Returning to the Scene of the Crime

By Mark Smedsrud

Mark Smedsrud grew up near the Big Sioux River in Sioux Falls, South Dakota. From his earliest fishing trips and other childhood adventures on the river, he always aspired to a career in wildlife. After graduating from South Dakota State University in 1986, his career began with South Dakota Game, Fish & Parks (SDGFP). He started as an animal damage control trapper in Sioux Falls before transitioning to a conservation officer position in Madison, South Dakota. From 1988 – 1990, Officer Smedsrud served Lake County before moving back to Sioux Falls and serving Minnehaha County. After approximately eight years as a field officer, Smedsrud took on a supervisory role and expanded his duties for the duration of his career. He retired from SDGFP in April 2013. He remains involved with the South Dakota Conservation Officers Association and is an avid outdoorsman.

A conservation officer's (CO's) duties change as the seasons change. During the spring and summer months, fishing and recreational boating enforcement are priorities. Obviously, during the fall and winter months hunting takes center stage.

South Dakota has always been well known as a world-class pheasant hunting destination. Thousands of resident and non-resident hunters participate in this season every year. For most Conservation Officers, pheasant hunters create the majority of enforcement activity.

However, South Dakota also has decent big game hunting opportunities – whitetail and mule deer, antelope and even elk. The majority of firearm licenses for these seasons are available to South Dakota residents only.

I spent my career stationed in eastern South Dakota. When I started as a CO, we had a 9-day firearm deer season that started in late November. Later, the season was extended to 16 days. The portion of the season that allowed only the harvest of antlerless deer was extended even longer. Those short 9-day seasons were full of activity for a CO. I noticed early in my career that many hunters seemed to put extra pressure on themselves to bag an animal during deer season.

This particular zeal didn't seem to apply to those hunting pheasants or waterfowl. It's possible it was the monetary cost of the tag. They felt by purchasing a deer tag, they were owed a freezer full of venison no matter what it took to get it. When you combined that type of pressure with a short season, it was interesting times for a CO to say the least!

During my first few years working deer seasons as a CO, I quickly learned why veteran officers referred to East River deer season as the "iron pony rodeo." The topography of southeastern South Dakota where I worked is generally flat. There are gravel township roads nearly every mile, surrounding every section of land. Using a high-powered rifle, most deer in a section would be within shooting range from the road. Many, if not most, deer hunters would simply drive around on the roads and in the fields with their 4-wheel drive trucks looking for deer. When a deer was spotted, the hunter might step out of the vehicle to shoot, or shoot out the window.

If the deer ran, the chase was on! Hunters would use the truck to chase the deer until they could get in to position to shoot, thus the term "iron pony rodeo."

Mind you, chasing deer is illegal. Shooting out the window of a vehicle is illegal. In most cases, shooting from the road is illegal.

I was shocked how prevalent this type of hunting activity was when I first started. But, as my career progressed, I accepted it as the norm. Some hunters just didn't seem to care that most activities combining hunting deer with motor vehicles were illegal – many did it anyway, even at the risk of losing their hunting privileges for a year or longer. Obviously, these activities yielded many complaints from the hunters trying to hunt legally and ethically.

As a young officer, my law enforcement supervisor gave me good advice about getting to know landowners and building relationships with the people in my county. He once told me if they knew and trusted me, they would call in violations. I found that to be very true and building relationships in the areas I worked was important. Later, when I became a supervisor myself, I gave the same advice to my officers.

The Big Sioux River runs north to south through Minnehaha County in eastern South Dakota. The corridor adjacent to the river is wooded and excellent deer habitat.

Mike was a landowner along the river and also an avid deer hunter. He managed his habitat for deer by providing food plots and undisturbed areas for the deer to live in. He harvested quality bucks every year with both firearm and archery tags.

I got to know Mike well early in my career – he had problems with hunters during deer season every year. There had even been deer poached at night within 100 yards of his house. On this particular day when I received his call, Mike was especially unhappy.

"Mark, I just had another deer poached on my property."

It was mid-week during the 9-day deer season. Mike was in his deer stand about 9 a.m. He had seen several deer that morning, but nothing he wanted to harvest. He was waiting for a nice 5x5 buck that he knew was living in the area.

As he sat, he heard the sound of a vehicle driving out on the adjacent road. It stopped. A single rifle shot rang out.

Mike was not shy about confronting hunters if given the opportunity. He hurried out of his tree stand and ran towards the sound of the shot. As he cleared the tree line, he saw a white Chevrolet pickup parked on the road with two men in it. The passenger window was rolled down. Mike yelled at the men, telling them to stay there. Not surprisingly, the truck quickly sped off.

I arrived at Mike's about 30 minutes after the incident occurred. As I mentioned, Mike was not particularly happy.

He had already searched the wooded area on his property adjacent to where the suspect truck was parked. He found the prized 5x5 buck he had been hunting for. It was dead and still warm, approximately 100 yards from the road where the suspect vehicle was parked. Ironically, it was only another 100 yards from where Mike had been sitting in his tree stand.

I examined the buck, which I estimated had about a 150-inch Boone & Crockett score, and discovered a single bullet wound. The round passed through the animal, making a bullet recovery impossible. There was no evidence to be had.

Mike and I drug the animal to the road and I took a statement from him, detailing what had happened that morning. Our only evidence was two men in a white Chevrolet pickup. I searched for a bullet casing where the vehicle was stopped but did not locate any.

I would have to take the deer to the evidence freezer. Mike and I were just preparing to load the deer into my patrol vehicle when a blue Ford pickup came driving up. It had two men in it.

The pair had on blaze orange clothing and were obviously hunters. They got out of the vehicle and looked at the deer. We made small talk about hunting and the unfortunate incident that had occurred at Mike's that morning.

Interestingly, they asked what would happen to the deer. One of the hunters then asked me if I would mind if he took a picture. It was such a magnificent animal, after all.

I told him to go ahead and have his photo. The two hunters left.

Mike and I loaded the deer. He expressed his frustration at the situation. Some hunters are willing to break every law to shoot a big buck, he said, but he was doing it the right way. And what did he have to show for it?

"You will probably never catch the SOB's either," he lamented. "There's such limited evidence available."

"We'll see," I told him. "It just might be solvable."

In fact, I thought our suspects had just left after taking pictures of the deer they shot (or, more specifically, poached) earlier that morning. They couldn't resist coming back for a look; they just thought it prudent to switch vehicles first.

Fortunately, I recorded the license number of the blue Ford pickup before they left.

Upon running the license plate number of the blue Ford pickup, I discovered the registered owner had been issued a Minnehaha County deer license for that year.

Later that evening, I went to the registered owner's house. When he answered the door, I looked him in the eye.

"You know why I'm here, don't you?" He looked down.

"Yes."

He proceeded to give a full confession.

The two had been driving down the road and saw the buck standing in the timber about 100 yards from the road. The hunter (poacher) shot the buck from the window of the truck on private property that he did not have permission to hunt. He and his companion would each be convicted of several charges.

The next day I stopped back at Mike's and informed him what had transpired.

It was one of the few times I ever saw him smile.

Deer Roping

By Jeff McEntee

Jeff McEntee began his career with South Dakota Game, Fish & Parks (SDGFP) as a conservation officer in 1991, stationed in Mitchell. In 2002, he became a wildlife investigator and retired in 2017.

The exact date and year escape me, but I'm certain it was in the early part of my career that I had the opportunity to rope a whitetail doe. Yes, you read that right – I roped a whitetail doe.

As time elapses, it seems the stories from my 26 years working in wildlife law enforcement tend to slip away. It's usually while rehashing old stories with fellow veterans that many of the interesting stories come back to me.

The life and death ones are always easy to recall and reflect upon. It's the "routine" ones that need a little bit of prodding to fully come back to my memory. It was during a conversation with fellow officers about injured wildlife situations that the story of an injured whitetail deer came back in full color.

The situation occurred sometime in the early fall of 1995 or 1996. I was on patrol in western Davison County during pheasant season. I received a message from the Mitchell Police Department regarding an injured deer. A group of pheasant hunters had come across her and something had to be done.

This seemed like just another call; I received many reports of injured animals as a conservation officer in Davison and Hanson Counties in eastern South Dakota. It was quite common to respond to injured wild birds and mammals, which suffered from a wide range of ailments.

We had little-to-no training on this subject in those days. The general idea was keeping your hands and fingers away from the business end of whichever animal was suffering. Most of this was accomplished by trial and error. To be honest, I had my fair share of errors!

Since I was familiar with the location of the landowner who was requesting assistance, I informed dispatch that I would be in route to his location and asked them to inform the landowner of the same. ETA, 25 minutes.

This is where I need to back up and talk about some of the training that prepared me for what was about to happen.

In 1993, I became a defensive tactics instructor with SDGFP. My responsibilities included traveling around the state to conduct the bi-annual training each law enforcement officer was required to attend two times a year. Because instructors were somewhat limited, we often traveled to other regions to provide assistance to their existing instructor cadre.

About a month prior to the aforementioned injured deer call, I found myself in the western Black Hills, helping that region with training for a couple of days. The training site was at a remote location in the timber and each officer stayed in a camper, tent or run-down cabin for the duration of the training.

The first evening, after dinner, two of the western officers unloaded a couple small square bales from the back of their patrol vehicles. Into one end of each bale went a plastic steer head.

This piqued my curiosity.

Then, each retrieved a lariat from their pickup and began to practice their roping skills on the stationary steer heads. Apparently, one of them noticed my interest and asked if I wanted to give it a try.

Being an East River officer – and the only one there for that matter – I decided to let them train me in the fine art of roping. I had seen it done on TV and even at the local rodeo in Mitchell on more than one occasion. But I had never held a lariat in my hands prior to that day.

They showed me how to hold it properly, as well as the correct method for rolling my wrists over my head to maintain the integrity of the loop. After a few tries, I got the hang of casting the rope and could eventually lasso the stationary steer head more times than I missed. Needless to say, I instantly had an appreciation for the cowboys at the rodeo who accomplished this task effortlessly – all while atop a moving horse pursuing a running steer.

I certainly wasn't ready for that…yet.

As I pulled into the landowner's driveway on that fall day, I was greeted by approximately 20 pheasant hunters in the yard. The landowner approached my vehicle and told me that the injured deer was behind his house, standing on the edge of a small pond.

"Follow me around back and I'll take you to the deer," he said.

As I agreed, one of the hunters approached and asked if he could ride with me. He told me he was a conservation officer from Minnesota and wanted to see how I handled the situation. I told him to jump in – he could possibly provide assistance.

As I followed the landowner around the tree strip behind his house, I immediately spotted the deer standing approximately 7-8 feet from the shore of the pond.

She was in about one foot of water and appeared to be sniffing the air around her. As I exited my vehicle about 30 yards from the deer, I could tell the deer had been shot in the face with a shotgun. She was obviously suffering, blinded in both eyes from the shotgun blast.

Unfortunately, at the time, the only remedy was to euthanize the animal. After surveying the situation for a minute, I turned back to retrieve my patrol rifle from behind the seat of my pickup. It was then I noticed the entire hunting party had walked through the trees. Everyone was watching from a short distance away. So, now I had an audience.

As I turned my attention back to the deer, I realized I did not have a set of rubber boots or waders with me to retrieve the deer once it was dispatched. Recalling my recent roping training in the Black Hills, I jokingly asked the landowner if he had a lariat.

I said this knowing full well that East River landowners never carry such a tool in their pickups…or so I thought.

The landowner immediately responded in the affirmative and walked over to his pickup, tilted forward the seat and removed a short piece of rope that at one time resembled a lariat.

Now, I spent a great deal of my youth on a farm. The "lariat" the landowner was showing me was more like a lead rope for horses or show cows. It possessed no rigidity, which is key to aid in the twirling and casting motions. To make matters worse it was, at most, 7 to 8 feet long.

Did I mention how far the deer was standing from the shore?

Holding the rope in my hands, I looked up and saw the crowd, filled with excitement. They had a front row seat to watch a South Dakota Conservation Officer rope a live deer.

I wasn't especially confident I could pull this one off.

In fact, I now faced the strong likelihood of becoming not only the laughing stock of eastern South Dakota, but an annual story for the hunting group for years to come.

It was then that I recalled a piece of advice a veteran officer once gave me: *when you're doing something with the public, even if it's your first time, act like you've done it a thousand times.*

Let the acting begin!

As I walked up to the edge of the pond, I realized I was still carrying my patrol rifle in my right hand. I laid the weapon on the ground in a safe, but accessible location.

Since I felt the rope was going to be very short for making the throw, I walked right up to the edge of the water. I tried a couple of times to twirl the rope to open the loop for casting, but it was just too limp to accomplish this with any regularity. After some adjustment to the size of the loop, on the third attempt, I was able to form a semblance of a loop over my head.

It was time to let it fly!

I let go of the rope with my right hand and held on with my left. Much to my surprise, the loop landed perfectly around the deer's neck. The Minnesota officer standing next to me shouted "you got her!"

Believe me when I say I was equally surprised.

I was so proud of myself for the accomplishment, I totally forgot that I now had a blind, adult deer on the end of a rope... which fully possessed all of its remaining faculties, including four very strong legs.

Needless to say, the fight was on!

As I was being dragged towards the water, the Minnesota officer yelled to me, inquiring whether I wanted him to grab my rifle and shoot the deer.

Due to several obvious safety concerns and, not knowing if this guy was an actual officer or not, I instructed him to leave the gun on the ground, all the while trying to give him the impression that I'd done this a thousand times before.

It's amazing the thoughts that go through your mind in life and death situations…

One I can recall is being drug across a pond by a blind deer while a couple dozen by-standers pass out from laughter.

Another is the deer turning around with the intent to stomp the ever-living stuffing out of whatever is keeping it from escape, again while a couple dozen by-standers pass out from laughter.

It was time to do something. Anything!

I instinctively drew my duty weapon from its holster and pointed it at the head of the flailing deer. While my left arm was practically being torn out of its socket, I was able to maintain a semblance of a sight picture and pulled the trigger.

The bullet found its mark and all activity ceased immediately.

I could hardly believe what had just transpired. I'm quite certain the look on my face confirmed my surprise. Fortunately, I was facing away from the crowd – they could only see the result of my actions and not my look of utter shock and disbelief.

I quickly composed myself and turned around to find the entire group giving me a standing ovation. (I realize they were probably standing to begin with, but it's my story and for all I know, while

I was roping and shooting, they were sitting down on the ground enjoying the show.)

After loading the deer into the back of my pickup and leaving the residence, I met up with one of my supervisors who happened to be patrolling in the same general area.

To say I was excited about what had just transpired would be a drastic understatement.

I relayed my story, blow by blow, from the blinded deer to the sorry excuse for the lariat to the single shot.

The look on his face said it all ... YEAH RIGHT!

I could tell he doubted my rendition of the story. I had to admit it could have easily been embellished. Over the next six years or so, I occasionally told the story to others. Most had the same doubtful expression my supervisor had that day.

Sometime later, in the early 2000's, I was at the annual Tri-State Conference. I had been asked to give a presentation about some recent work I had done on commercial poaching cases in my new role as a wildlife investigator.

With officers attending from South Dakota, Minnesota and Iowa, the Tri-State Conference allowed for information sharing on issues related to wildlife law enforcement in bordering states.

After my talk, I was milling about the crowd during the break between speakers when one of the officers approached me. He identified himself as the Minnesota officer who had witnessed the deer roping. I quickly led him to a group of my doubters and asked him to repeat the story to them. I stood away from the group – but within earshot – as they gathered around him to hear his version of the story.

It was exactly the same.

No Piece of Information Too Small

By Chad Williams

Chad Williams began his career with South Dakota Game, Fish and Parks in 2003 as a park ranger stationed out of Palisades State Park. In 2005, Chad made the switch from the Parks Division to the Wildlife Division and became the conservation officer stationed out of Flandreau in Moody County. Chad graduated from South Dakota State University with a bachelor's degree in Wildlife and Fisheries Sciences and a minor in Criminal Justice. Chad has been on the South Dakota Conservation Officers Association (SDCOA) board since 2007 and has been the Region 3 representative for several years. He served as vice president, president for four years, and is currently filling the role of past president on the board.

Early on in my career as a conservation officer I learned that any bit of information could be valuable – it didn't matter if it came through the Turn In Poachers (TIPs) hotline or directly to me. Even the smallest tidbit of information can lead to big cases. As a young officer, I learned quickly how valuable investigation skills are to making or breaking a case, as well as how helpful veteran officers can be with their experiences. Most of the time, it is not easy to piece together the puzzle of just what happened in any given scenario.

My first big deer case started out with just a tidbit of information. It was the fall of 2006 when I found a dead deer lying along the side of the roadway in Moody County. The head was gone, cut clean off at the neck.

It was a very large-bodied deer and I immediately wondered how large the rack must have been… it was likely impressive.

First of all, I had to determine if, in fact, the deer had been poached or if it was a car/deer accident. If it was an accident, it was still illegal for someone to remove the head of the animal. Most people don't realize it's a crime to remove the antlers of a roadkill deer, thinking "it's only roadkill."

There are some instances when antlers can be kept after a deer is killed in an accident, but not in every case and the requirements are strict.

Examining the deer carcass, I discovered one bullet wound in the chest cavity that went clean through. This deer had been poached and I had no possibility of recovering a bullet.

So, what do I do now? Where do I start?

With advancing technology and the potential to use DNA, dealing with a situation like this is like processing a crime scene. Photographs are taken, GPS coordinates recorded and tissue samples saved for DNA matching. Next, I needed to find some leads – someone out there had knowledge of this poached deer.

I turned to farmers in the area, as well as sportsmen. There was one bow hunter in particular who was an avid sportsman and spent many hours in tree stands. I knew Rex was familiar with quite a few of the larger bucks in the area.

A couple of months went by after I initially contacted him, but Rex turned out to be my next source of information.

When Rex called, he provided just what I needed. A hunter I will refer to as Longford brought the head of a very large buck to a taxidermist in the Sioux Falls area… Just the head.

Rex did a little investigating of his own while he was at the taxidermist's shop. He inquired about the buck – where had it been taken and what was the story behind it?

It turned out that Longford had brought the deer head into the taxidermist to have the rack officially scored. He was telling everyone he shot the buck in Moody County. Longford had described the general area where my headless deer showed up… "Here we go!" I thought… I was sure I had caught my big break, this had to be the buck.

I continued to dig up all the information I could on Longford, including past hunting violations and current licenses. Longford had some criminal history and past hunting violations, but nothing too major. He also had a valid rifle deer license for Moody County. I thought I was definitely on the right track.

I talked with the taxidermist and thought it was time to knock on Longford's door to see what he had to say. I brought along fellow Conservation Officer Shawn Wichmann to help with the interview.

We were two eager and motivated rookie game wardens. Longford appeared to be expecting us, which is never good. It's always nice to catch them by surprise and give them less time to think up a story. I suspected the taxidermist contacted Longford and gave us away.

Longford played it cool at first, as if he hadn't done anything wrong. But soon, his body language said otherwise. Longford was giving us bits and pieces of the truth and leaving out the important details. Shawn and I managed to get our hands on a deer rack located in his garage. It was a very large rack, with a gross Boone and Crocket score in the 190's.

We were glad to finally see the rack and take photos for evidence. Shawn and I continued to work on obtaining the truth from Longford. We were ever-so-close, but could not seal the deal.

After our conversation with Longford, Shawn and I went to work tracking down his friends and conducting several more interviews to try and piece together what really happened.

After several hours spent on this case and numerous contacts made, we still did not have enough to move forward with prosecution.

Oh, we were close!

We both knew Longford poached this deer, but we couldn't prove it yet. I didn't have quite enough information to seize the deer rack and test for a DNA match. But I knew. My game warden instincts told me that Longford poached this buck. Maybe not the area I had initially thought, but I just knew he poached it.

I was not giving up. I had the mindset that I was never giving up on this one and something would turn up.

In the spring of 2007, several months after I first found the deer with the missing head, Longford entered his buck into a big buck contest at a sports show. I just happened to be working it. Unfortunately, I also happened to run into Longford. He was very sure to let me know his trophy was up on the big buck display.

I kindly told Longford that our investigation was not over. "You just wait," I thought to myself.

In January 2008, more than a year after finding the headless deer in Moody County, our department received new information from the TIPs hotline through an email. The email was sent out region-wide because the staffer who received it didn't know what area or case this information pertained to.

But I sure did.

As soon as I read this TIPs information, I knew it was my case and I was all fired up again. The investigation was reopened and I was ready. I made sure I was prepared for round two.

You see, enough time had passed that our friend Longford had talked about this particular buck with too many people. His story was eventually heard by an individual who was not happy with how Longford shot this buck, so they reported it.

Bragging will get you every time.

The new information provided in the email was substantial and revealed where the buck was shot. It was not shot in Moody County and, in fact, was not even related to the headless buck that started the investigation – it was not the same deer.

Instead, this deer was shot in Minnehaha County – in Sioux Falls, within city limits, under cover of darkness in the early morning hours. The information also confirmed our suspicions about who helped Longford retrieve the buck – one of his close friends, Tyler.

I interviewed Tyler and, again, I was very close to obtaining the truth. Just not close enough. Tyler's body language was telling me he did it, but his words were not. I simply was not far enough along in my career yet – I did not have enough training or experience with interviews to get Tyler to confess. I thanked Tyler and kindly asked him if he would be willing to meet with me again in the event that I had any other questions. He agreed.

At this point, I looked to one of my role models and mentors, who was also my supervisor, Mark Smedsrud. He was a wealth of knowledge and experience. I learned a great deal from him and this case was a prime example of one of the times I learned the most.

Smedsrud was aware of my progress and was more than willing to accompany me on an interview with Tyler. Smedsrud and I met with

Tyler at his residence and the plan was to take a drive out to where Tyler and Longford claimed this buck was shot in Moody County.

At this point in the investigation, both Smedsrud and I were well aware the buck in question was never shot in Moody County.

Smedsrud built rapport and trust with Tyler and, without giving away too many of his tactics, he gained a full confession. This was a turning point for me early in my career. I saw very clearly how important interview and communication skills are in our line of work; they are what make great investigations and, eventually, great cases.

After obtaining the confession from Tyler things just snowballed. I was able to find more acquaintances of Longford's who had knowledge of his poached buck. Eventually, the situation reached a breaking point – Longford simply could not stand it any longer and contacted me to confess.

I still remember very well the day I was able to return to Longford's residence and seize the trophy rack he had taken illegally. Even though it wasn't the headless deer from Moody County, it was well worth all the work and effort we put in.

This case just goes to show how a little tidbit of information can turn into something a whole lot bigger with a little persistence and patience. Even though I did not solve the initial case this all stemmed from, it sure lead to bigger and better things.

Not only did Longford confess to illegally killing a trophy buck, but he also gave us information on his friend Tyler. Longford ended up with multiple charges, but his buddy Tyler also ended up with charges and lost a large mule deer buck trophy he poached from the roadway during the West River deer season. They both lost their hunting privileges for a year.

Chad Williams is pictured with the trophy
from his first big deer case.

Longford's trophy deer rack is currently located in our TIPs trailer. It travels around the state to different events and is on display as a reminder of what can happen when you make poor decisions. It is also a thank you to those individuals who care enough to report violations like this one and make the TIPs hotline a valuable resource to protect wildlife.

Without the help of our TIPs callers, we would not have been able to catch these poachers. Over the 16 years I have been in wildlife law enforcement, I have been able to resolve several cases and catch several poachers because of the sportsmen and sportswomen, landowners, ranchers, farmers and citizens who chose to make that call.

Adventures at Orman Dam

Mike Apland graduated from Chadron State College with a degree in Biological Sciences. He began his career with South Dakota Game, Fish & Parks in 1991, stationed in Britton. There was no formal "new guy" training at that time, so he learned from neighboring wardens. He recalls that "some of it was by the book, some not so much." Mike transferred to Spearfish in 1997 and became a supervisor in 2012.

Over the years, I have spent many a night patrolling Orman Dam with fellow warden Scott Mikkelson. It could be a wild and crazy place, especially prior to its eventual state park development on the south side.

One of these nights, as we were patrolling together near the boat ramp in the late-night hours, we saw an older 3-wheeler pull up to the bathrooms. Two visibly drunk individuals stumbled off the machine. We pulled up as the first individual exited the restroom and made contact.

We informed the individual he would no longer be operating that machine in his state of intoxication.

"I understand," he slurred. "Because I'm drunk. But my buddy, he's hammered."

When the other individual came out, they had a little meeting of the minds. Finally, they staggered over to us and asked if they could *push* the 3-wheeler back to camp.

"Sure, as long as you are not driving it," we told them.

The two started to push, but quickly realized this was not going to work. It might have been due to their state of intoxication. Or their apparent lack of physical conditioning. Or both.

So, in their bright minds they came up with a better plan... They would start the machine and, as one of them ran the throttle from alongside, the other would push from behind.

They started it up and the rocket scientist alongside goosed the throttle. We heard the roar of the engine and two drunken screams.

As the 3-wheeler went over the horizon, we could see them still hanging on – one being dragged to the side, still holding on to the handle bars and the second one being dragged behind, his pants now down to his ankles, bare butt shining in the moon light.

After our laughing had subsided a bit, I turned to Scott.

"What you think we should do now?"

In his infinite wisdom he said, "I think it's a good time to go home."

Another time I was at Orman, again with Scott Mikkelson, but this time we were on the water conducting boating safety checks. We pulled up to a boat with two older folks fishing.

They both looked weathered by a hard life and too much sun through the years. We started the conversation with chit chat and then I explained we were conducting boating safety checks.

I asked if we could see a couple floatation devices. I quickly learned I should have been more specific and asked for life jackets.

"What do you fellas need to see?" the gentleman asked, just as his companion proceeded to lift up her shirt.

"I think they want to see my boobs," she said.

As Scott and I quickly tried to turn our heads away, the gentlemen spoke up.

"Put them things away! I'm pretty sure they don't want to see that."

We had a chuckle and left them without completing the rest of our boat check.

I had a rancher complaining about "those damn eagles" eating all his turkeys.

"Are they bald eagles?" I asked.

"No," he said. "Not the bald ones, these are the ones with the big white heads."

Busted by Social Media: When Poachers Share the Evidence

Andy Petersen began his career with South Dakota Game, Fish & Parks in January 2002 and has been stationed in Mitchell for his entire career. He grew up in eastern Iowa and went to Upper Iowa University for his degree in Wildlife and Fisheries Sciences.

"I always wanted to be a game warden," said Andy. "When I finished college, they were hiring in South Dakota, so you have to go where you can get a job. It's pretty competitive."

One of the most bizarre cases Andy has ever worked began to unfold after he received a phone call about a stolen deer.

"I was sitting there, across a field and I literally *watched* this guy steal the buck out of the back of my pickup," the landowner told Andy on the phone.

"Are you sure?" Andy asked, not sure he was believing what he was hearing.

A landowner in Andy's area had been out hunting that morning and harvested a beautiful 5x5 whitetail buck.

"He still had a doe tag to fill, so he went back out hunting," recalls Andy. "He left the buck in the back of his pickup. His property borders some railroad tracks, so he told me he backed the truck in, making the deer more difficult to see if people drove by on the road."

The hunter was several hundred yards from his truck when he saw a 4-wheeler driving down the railroad tracks… the tracks he thought would protect his buck from being spotted from the road.

"He watched as the guy on the 4-wheeler stopped and circled back around to look at the deer, which is fairly common. People like to look at deer like this."

But then he got off the 4-wheeler.

He wrestled the deer out of the back of the truck and loaded it on the 4-wheeler… And he drove away.

"Being several hundred yards away, the landowner couldn't do anything but watch," said Andy. "When he got back to his truck, he was able to follow the 4-wheeler tracks on the gravel road for quite a ways, but then it turned to a paved road that went into town. That's when he called me."

It was already dark so Andy called the police department and asked them to keep an eye out for the deer and a blue 4-wheeler.

"We found out later that the guy who took the deer lived pretty near the landowner and the location the deer was take from. He was long home before anyone even started looking for him."

They had nothing to go on except a blue 4-wheeler.

With so little information, Andy used all the resources available to him.

"We decided to use Crime Stoppers and put out a bulletin the next day," said Andy. "These go out to radio stations and newspapers in the community."

It worked – they received a tip two days later.

"A guy at the Yamaha dealership called. Someone had come in with a blue 4-wheeler asking for an estimate on fixing the breaks. He noticed the back of the rig was covered in blood and deer hair. When he heard the alert, he called it in."

It's a small world, though. When Andy tracked down the name of the guy with the blue 4-wheeler, he realized he knew the family.

"I knew this guy's parents pretty well," said Andy. "That was a good thing, because he was kind of hard to track down. He didn't really have an address and spent a lot of time sleeping on other people's couches."

But his Facebook page was open to anyone who wanted to look at it.

"It turned out that he saw fit to post pictures of the deer, bragging that he had shot it," Andy said.

The picture posted on Facebook and the picture the landowner had taken showed the distinct, curving brow tine on the deer. They were a match.

After gathering more information, Andy figured out where the guy worked and went to question him.

"When I spoke to him, his story was that his boss had shot the deer and given it to him," said Andy. "On Facebook, he said he had shot it. Right there, we had conflicting stories."

Andy then spoke to the boss and told him what his employee had said.

"That made the boss really mad because he had no license," said Andy. "When he saw how mad boss was, he fessed up and told the whole story."

The deer thief was eventually charged with unlawful possession and had to pay fines and restitution totaling nearly $3,000.

"I would say it's the most bizarre case I've ever worked," said Andy. "I'd never heard of anything like it. I don't understand why someone would blatantly steal a nice deer just to brag about having it."

Andy has also received tips that came from other social media platforms to make a couple of cases.

"A guy shot two deer and shared it with his friends," said Andy. "The informant called me and told me about the video – the guy was bragging that he shot two deer with one shot *and* didn't have a license. Of course, the video is time stamped. And you could hear his voice saying 'two deer with one shot.'"

The evening turned out a series of shares – the shooter didn't stop with the first announcement.

From the details provided by his informant, Andy had a name and an address. He also knew they guy he was looking for, Christopher, didn't have any hunting licenses at all.

"On the way to Christopher's house, I got another photo from the informant of Christopher field dressing the deer," said Andy. "From the time Christopher sent the picture of himself skinning the deer to when I showed up at his house, only about 30 minutes had passed. Things moved very quickly that night."

Conservation Officer Lynn Geuke went with Andy to the residence. When they arrived, Christopher and his friend had just finished skinning and quartering the deer.

"Christopher was with another guy who had licenses," recalls Andy. "Christopher's story was that he took the rifle and shot because the guy with the license couldn't see the deer."

Christopher's friend had a different story. With new details, they re-interviewed Christopher.

"There were tags present, but they never put any tags on the deer at all," said Andy. "I don't believe they were going to. The deer were already quartered by the time we got there."

With violations established, the officers set about seizing the deer and the rifle used to poach them.

"They were upset about the deer, but when we told them we were taking the rifle, we nearly came to blows. I was glad Lynn was there and I wasn't alone with them."

By this time, Christopher's father had come out of the house.

"He was intoxicated and mad about the kids getting tickets," recalled Andy. "Then Christopher got mad about having the gun seized – he was yelling at us not to touch it."

Lynn went to the driver's side door to retrieve the gun. When he did, Christopher opened the passenger door in an attempt to beat him to it.

Thinking quickly, Andy kicked the door shut and warned Christopher that if he tried anything further, he would be going to jail.

"He was really close to fighting and getting arrested because he didn't want the gun seized," said Andy. "It was a tense situation, but we were able to talk them down and get out of there safely."

In the end, Christopher was charged with several violations, including killing two deer without a license and shooting from the road. He would pay $4800 in fines and be sentenced to 30 days in jail, though the jail time was suspended.

"The most interesting part about this case was that it came through social media and how fast we were able to respond," said Andy. "I got the tip at 5:30 and we were at his house by 8 p.m. He did all the work for me by taking pictures at every stage. I received up-to-the-minute, time stamped video with voice and locations."

Bridging Cultures in South Dakota

Chris began his career with South Dakota Game, Fish & Parks in 2010, just two months after graduating from Colorado State University with a degree in Natural Resource Management and a minor in Fish Biology. He was stationed in Huron before transferring to Sioux Falls.

Chris Kuntz worked in Huron for seven years at the start of his career as a conservation officer. During this time, the population in the east-central South Dakota town was changing. The farming community was becoming more diverse as Karen (pronounced *Kuh-ren*) people were moving there with the help of Lutheran Social Services.

"They were refugees," explains Chris. "They came from Myanmar and the region was – is still – in a state of civil war. Some of the elders had actually fought against the government there. Some of the Karen people I met had only ever lived in refugee camps. A few of them received a little education about western lifestyle from missionaries in the camps, but it was very minimal. A few people spoke some English, but most were not able to speak English at all; they had no clue about life in the United States."

In their homeland, the Karen had essentially lived off the land.

"They had no familiarity with hunting or fishing laws," said Chris. "It didn't take long for calls to start coming in regarding Karen people. Whether there were actual violations, or someone saw something unusual or alarming, the dynamics of two very different cultures coming together was a challenge. It was a hard situation for everyone."

Food preparation was a good example of the cultural divide.

"I received calls telling me about fish or some other animal hanging from a clothesline," said Chris. "Karen families would dry the meat for prep and storage. It was simply the way they did things – splitting it open and hanging it up to dry in the sun."

While it wasn't illegal, it was an unusual sight for neighbors.

"I also got many reports of deer being taken out of season that turned out to be hogs being processed in the garage or backyard," said Chris. "They did the butchering themselves. As part of this process, they would singe the fur or feathers from animals being butchered. Again, not illegal, but alarming to the neighbors."

On these calls, Chris tried to help them understand the neighbors weren't used to seeing things like this, but also tried to talk to them and learn something about their culture.

"One family shared with me that they were assigned the responsibility to bring a hog for the Karen new year's celebration," said Chris "They even invited me to attend."

After Chris's visits, families doing butchering tried to be discreet by closing the garage door most of the way. But Chris wasn't the only one receiving calls. Uncomfortable and confusing situations were occurring all over the community.

"Huron started a 'welcome to America' crash course," said Chris. "Classes were held every month and covered things like banking, how to secure housing, finding a job and applying for a driver's license or identification. In any given class, there would be 2-12 people, most of whom had been in the United States for less than a month."

The police department also helped with the classes and Chris talked about fish and game laws.

"Often times, they hadn't been in the community long enough to really grasp what I was talking about," he said. "There were a lot of women who attended, who then brought the information home to their husbands and children. They were always very thankful for the information and tried to do the right thing."

Providing education was the right thing to do, but the education would need to go both ways to truly make a connection.

"I really tried to learn about their culture and understand where they were coming from," said Chris. "I learned that they came from Myanmar, also known as Burma, in southeast Asia. There are seven different subcultures from the region, including Karen, Hmong, Burmese and Chen. In Huron, it was about 95% Karen. There were four Hmong families, one lady was Chen and there were a couple Burmese and a couple Thai."

What was more challenging was that each group spoke their own dialect – they did not understand one another.

"Thai was kind of the common denominator," said Chris. "We were working a case once and needed an interpreter. A man who was Thai helped us. The people we needed to communicate with didn't understand entirely, but we got through enough to at least help them understand what was going on."

Along with the city's efforts, Conservation Officer Andy Petersen from Mitchell held a class about fishing with the help of an officer from the Minnesota Department of Natural Resources and a leader from a Karen organization, also in Minnesota.

"The leader of the Karen organization helped a number of us officers learn more about the Karen people," said Chris. "This initial class gave way to a couple other fishing classes because many of them were participating in fishing at the time. As the years went by, more and more Karen started venturing into hunting. This led to a hunting class for the Karen which ultimately changed into a full HuntSAFE class."

The classes proved beneficial, as did Chris's efforts to learn what he could about their culture and language. Education was the key to bridging the two cultures.

"We had close to 200 people go through those three or four hunting classes," he said. "So many people showed up the first night, we about blew the doors off the church basement!"

They knew they had reached a turning point one day when Chris's supervisor, Mark Smedsrud, came to town after the first hunting class had taken place.

"We were out in the field and came across a group of Karen people," recalls Chris. "Smedsrud pointed at a duck and asked the guy 'what's this and how many can you have?'"

The man got out his ID book, found the duck and answered that he could have three.

"He was correct!" said Chris. "Our efforts were working. We were providing education and the people we were trying to reach were getting it."

Another day, Chris ran across a Karen man who had become his friend. He was out hunting and explained to Chris that he was having a problem.

"Mark Smedsrud was with me again that day," recalls Chris. "Moses was hunting with two other friends who spoke no English at the time, but he was almost fluent."

Moses knew he needed a plug in his shotgun, but didn't know where to get one or how to put one in.

"He told me he compensated by making sure they put only two shells in the gun at a time," said Chris. "He was really trying to do the right thing. I showed him how to make a plug and also let him know where he could buy one."

Soon, Chris was getting calls from other areas in the state from officers starting to meet Karen people out in the field.

"They were calling to say these folks were out doing the right thing," said Chris. "That was a great feeling."

Chris focused on providing education to the Karen people in his community because he felt it was the right thing to do.

"Punishing them wasn't going to help," he said. "What they were doing was not intentional. Education was imperative. When they had an opportunity to learn what was right, they did it. And we built some great relationships while we helped our community. Everyone benefitted."

As time passed, many of the cultural difference calls started to subside. Everyone was adjusting to the differences in cultures – from both sides.

"It was fun to see the Karen people change over time as well," said Chris. "They went from mainly sticking to their community to becoming more and more involved in school sports and activities. They even started dressing up at Halloween to go trick or treating."

Chris worked hard to provide extra education for the Karen people in his community and he would do it again.

"It was the right thing to do, to help them out by teaching classes," said Chris. "There's a time and a place for a ticket, but if the people receiving the citation don't understand that what they did was wrong or *why* it was wrong, nothing changes."

About the Author:

Jona Ohm has lived in Lyman County, South Dakota, for 15 years, where her husband Mark served as a conservation officer. As a hunter and sportswoman, she is grateful for the dedication and passion these officers feel for their work. As the wife of an officer, she knows firsthand what it's like to be waiting at home.

A writer all her life, Jona earned her bachelor's degree at Northern State University in Aberdeen, South Dakota and her master's degree at the University of Wollongong in New South Wales, Australia. While Mark is out protecting wildlife, she dedicates her time and talent to the children and families served by St. Joseph's Indian School.